Benjamin Franklin

Books by Clara Ingram Judson

Abraham Lincoln, Friend of the People
Admiral Christopher Columbus (1965)
Andrew Carnegie
Andrew Jackson, Frontier Statesman
Benjamin Franklin
Bruce Carries the Flag
George Washington, Leader of the People
The Lost Violin
Michael's Victory
The Mighty Soo
Mr. Justice Holmes
Petar's Treasure
Pierre's Lucky Pouch
Reaper Man, The Story of Cyrus Hall McCormick
St. Lawrence Seaway
Sod-House Winter
Theodore Roosevelt, Fighting Patriot
Thomas Jefferson, Champion of the People
Yankee Clippers, The Story of Donald McKay (1965)

For Younger Readers

Abraham Lincoln
Christopher Columbus
George Washington

Benjamin Franklin

by Clara Ingram Judson

Illustrated by Robert Frankenberg

FOLLETT PUBLISHING COMPANY · CHICAGO · NEW YORK

Library of Congress Catalog Card Number: 57-11030

SEVENTH PRINTING

Follett Publishing Company
1010 West Washington Boulevard
Chicago, Illinois   60607

TL 0745

Author's Foreword

Benjamin Franklin's life was too full and varied to put in one book — his versatile personality, his mighty accomplishments, defy the limitations of a single volume. I have not attempted an inclusive biography; instead I have told about his work for his country and enough of his personal life and accomplishments to show how it came about that he, more than any other man of his time, was fitted to stand firm against England; to get essential help from France, Holland, and Spain; and, after military victory was won, to help the new nation achieve unity under a new constitution.

As I think over the many kind and skilled people who aided my research, my gratitude goes to Mrs. Carolyn W. Field, Coordinator, Work with Children, in The Free Library of Philadelphia, who arranged appointments for me with Franklin scholars now working in Philadelphia. She thus opened doors for me to a rich new area of knowledge and understanding.

Among the scholars I met in this way I am indebted to Dr. Edwin Wolf, 2nd, Librarian, The Library Company of Philadelphia (the original Junto library), who generously shared with me his knowledge of James Logan and the vital influence Logan and his library had upon Franklin; to Dr. Whitfield J. Bell, Jr., Associate Editor of *The Papers of Benjamin Franklin,* who guided my study on several points; to Dr. William H. McCarthy, Curator, Rosenbach Foundation Museum, who allowed me to read the only known copy of the first "Poor Richard" *Almanac,* and several other invaluable copies of the almanac, as well as Madame Brillon's precious letter about the whistle. Mrs. Field also arranged with Mr. Albert D. Hollingsworth my visit to the Franklin Institute, where Mrs. Sue Collins showed me Franklin treasures and gave me invaluable new material.

In addition to these, I am indebted to Mr. George B. Fairchild of the Historical Society of Pennsylvania (with whom I had worked on Washington and Jefferson) ; to several persons at the American Philosophical Society; to Miss Harriet Swift of the Boston Public Library (with whom I had worked on Washington and Holmes), who assembled a quantity of choice material on Franklin's Boston years; to Mr. Donald L. LaChance, Evanston, who generously loaned me old and rare books about Franklin; to Dr. Felix Pollak, Rare Book Room, Deering Library, Northwestern University, who allowed me to read the first edition (1727) of Defoe's *Complete English Tradesman;* to The Society of Colonial Dames for information and a picture of Stenton; and, as always, to my friends in the Evanston Public Library.

Perhaps my deepest debt is to Ben himself, for the autobiography he wrote in England, far away from his treasured letters and records. Ben was sixty-five when he penned this work to tell his son family facts he wanted William to know. Today it is included in every well chosen library as the best autobiography in English literature and a treasure-store for one who would know Ben Franklin.

C.I.J.

May 2, 1957

Benjamin Franklin

The Candlemaker's Son

A cool sea breeze drifted over Boston Bay and the Long Wharf. It wafted up Union Street and swayed the sign of the Blue Ball hanging in front of Josiah Franklin's soap and candle shop. It came to the shed where he poured hot tallow into candle molds.

Josiah set aside the empty can, went to the door and enjoyed the breeze. His son Ben did not look up from work—measuring candlewicks by a mark on the bench and cutting even lengths. He had learned how to do two things at the same moment: cut wicks and think of the sea.

Ben loved the water. He would never forget the day they'd moved from the Milk Street house where he was born to this place at Union and Hanover.

"You boys have worked hard," his mother had said. "Run down to the Mill Pond and cool off." She pointed down the hill to the left of Union Street. "Yes, you may go, too, Ben, but you older boys must watch him." Ben was five then, but he

Learn of the skillful;
he that teaches himself
hath a fool for a master.

loved the water from that first day. Now, when he was ten, he could swim backward and forward; he could float, tread water, and dive from a sort of pier of logs, above the mud.

But this day he was not thinking about the Mill Pond, nor the thick smell of tallow on an August day, nor his growing pile of wicks.

"Breeze feels good, doesn't it, Ben?" Josiah Franklin remarked.

"It comes from the sea," Ben said. "Father, I'd like to go to sea!" There! The words were spoken.

"Ben!" Josiah whirled around and stared at his son. "Don't say that! It is sad enough that your brother Josiah, my own name-sake, ran away to sea and is not heard from yet! I cannot bear it that you, too, talk of the sea." He glanced at the pile of neat, even wicks Ben had cut. "You dream of the sea because the day is hot," he said kindly. "Tie those wicks into the molds while I melt another batch of tallow. Then you may have a swim. You'll like that."

"Thank you, Father. And may I go to the Long Wharf, too? Peter says a ship from the East may be in today. I'd like to see it."

Josiah Franklin nodded permission as he spooned hunks of tallow into the kettle and built up the fire till it roared. The smell of melting fat lay heavy in the shed.

Ben hardly noticed. His deft fingers tied wicks till the molds were ready. Then he dashed out to the street, hoping to find a companion. From the corner, he could look across toward the Long Wharf and the Bay. A ship was arriving now! The same breeze that had refreshed Ben and his father was bringing the handsome vessel toward the wharf—there was no time for a swim! Ben dashed down Union Street without a glance at the apothecary's shop windows. He ran out onto the wharf just in time to catch one of the ropes sailors tossed ashore. The rope made fast, Ben climbed onto a piling, steadied himself with his bare toes, and watched strange, swarthy men with dangling gold earrings unload cargo. They seemed healthy, not exhausted by toil—Josiah always told Ben sailors were overworked. They sang in a strange, exciting tongue as they carried bales and barrels down the narrow gangplank.

I shall go to sea, Ben thought. But perhaps I shall wait for a time. Sailors are grown men, that I can see.

As he watched the stir and confusion, Ben spied a small round object drop from a sack and roll on the wharf. He slid down and picked it up. A nutmeg—should he return it? He ran to the gangplank.

"Captain! Captain!" he shouted. The officers paid no heed. A sailor carrying a keg smiled and nodded. Did that mean Ben could keep his find? His mother would prize it. A year or more ago a neighbor had been given a nutmeg. She had planted it and now had a little tree, in bloom and promising a few tiny nuts. Ben grinned back at the sailor and put the nut in his pocket, sure that he was allowed to have it.

A bell rang aboard ship.

"They're going to have supper," a neighbor playmate said. "Let's go swimming."

Ben eyed the water of the Bay with longing—it was so deep and blue and cool. Bears often swam across that Bay; sometimes sailors shot a bear for fresh meat. But boys were not allowed. However, the Mill Pond was near. Boys who had been watching the ship dashed around the hill, jerked off their clothes, and plunged in, splashing.

As Ben dived from the well balanced log that served as a pier he thought of the mud beneath that log—a person couldn't dive from mud. He came up and rubbed water from his eyes, thinking of the stone wharf that he had once proposed to build. The boys had admired his daring but doubted his ability. Ben remembered the talk perfectly.

"Where'll you get the stone?" one had said.

Ben looked around. "There's stone over there."

"That's stone for a house, Ben. You know that."

"It's for our wharf." Ben spoke so convincingly that soon the boys were helping him carry the heavy stones and make a wharf. The work finished, they sat in a row and splashed bare feet in the clean water.

The next morning workmen came to lay the foundation for that new house. They missed their stone — and saw the wharf. Since the workmen were neighbors, they went straight to certain fathers. . . .

Ben often chuckled when he recalled how three boys rubbed their bottoms as the four of them lugged back stones. He was the only one who stood straight—and did not grumble.

"Didn't your father beat you?" one lad asked enviously.

"My father convinced me that the stones were for that house," Ben said. Even at eight years, Ben Franklin had a sense of personal dignity; what happened was between his father and himself and was their own business. A few days later, Josiah Franklin, who had not noticed the mud before, got help and laid logs over the mud. So Ben's idea worked, though in a different way than he had planned. That must have been two summers ago, after Ben had left Grammar School.

Now he stood tall and turned a graceful somersault into the pond.

A few days after the ship came in, Ben was sent to deliver
candles. He carried several orders of a dozen each—good
business for summer; most people simply went to bed at dark
and saved the cost of candles. On his return Ben found his
father sitting on a bench in the shade, deep in thought.

"Ben, I'm sorry," Josiah said, "but I cannot afford to send
you to school, come winter."

Ben was astonished at his father's serious tone and manner.

"Don't fret yourself, Father," he said hastily. "School
doesn't matter. You know I failed in ciphering when you sent
me to Master Brownwell last winter. He was a good master and
tried harder than I did. And as for Latin—I have no hanker
for Latin, Father."

"I meant for you to be a minister, Ben." Franklin shook
his head sadly. "You are my tenth son. I meant you to be my
tithe to the Lord."

"I am not sure that I'd like to write a sermon every week,
Father," Ben consoled. "Sermons are dull reading. I have read
more than half the books on your shelf—all sermons. And I
have read many that Uncle Benjamin sent from England. *Pilgrim's Progress* that Mr. Bunyan wrote is more interesting."

"Where did you get that book?" Josiah asked, suddenly
erect. "Did you show it to me?"

"Not yet, Father. I got it only yesterday, and you had a
visitor last evening. It is exciting, Father. People talk to each
other—Christian, Obstinate, Mercy—there are many charac-
ters. When I read, they seem real; not sermons." Ben's eyes
glowed. The novelty of conversation in a book had charmed

him into reading until the last drop of his candle burned up.

"How did you get the book?" Franklin asked. "Is it new?"

"Oh, no, Father. It's quite old, but it reads as well as new. I bought it with the pennies Mr. Archer gave me for carrying his market basket Tuesday."

"You like to read." Franklin seemed relieved about school. "Likely you can get some learning from books. But you are not to talk of the sea—understand?"

"Yes, Father."

"For the now, you are to help here. When you are twelve, I shall try to find a trade you like and apprentice you to learn it." Comforted by the way Ben accepted this decision, Franklin went into the house. Ben dashed off for the Mill Pond.

Ben's life was pleasant enough during those next two years—1716 to 1718. Josiah Franklin was an intelligent man; he had many friends. Often he asked one or two of these to supper and an evening of music or talk. Josiah played the violin and had a good voice for leading singing. On other evenings, talk ranged widely.

Food was very plain. The children were taught to eat what was set before them.

"I give you the best food we have today," Mrs. Franklin would say. "If you do not like it, think of something else while you eat." With a family of seventeen children, ten or twelve

usually gathered around the table even though some of the older children were married and away. Josiah Franklin's income was strained enough to buy simple food, clothes, and shoes for winter without the added cost of school for Ben.

From talk at the table, Ben picked up facts about his father. Josiah had been trained as a dyer of silk, in England. But when he moved to Massachusetts, he found that few people wore silk. Fortunately he knew how to make soap and candles—simple things that many people needed. So he made a living.

But most of the talk was about events, not people. Boston had many great fires; there had been a terrible one in 1711, the year the Franklins moved from the Milk Street house to this larger place, where they prospered in spite of the fire that brought disaster to many. There was talk of witchcraft. Though it was some years since the last witch had been put to death in nearby Salem, the topic was still good. Perhaps the liveliest talk was about banks; it was said someone wanted to start a bank in Boston.

"An evil thing, a bank," one of Mr. Franklin's friends said.

"It would encourage debt. Why should I loan money that I save to a bank who will loan it out? Let men save their own, I say."

"Probably nothing will come of it but talk," Josiah said, when tempers began to grow hot. He liked discussion but not argument.

At the end of the table, Ben listened. I shall save *my* money for books, he decided. Later he sold *Pilgrim's Progress;* he had read it so often that he knew it well. With the money he bought

some historical leaflets. By buying and selling he increased his
knowledge from books, ranging widely, reading anything he
could buy.

In this same period, he began writing long letters to Uncle
Benjamin Franklin in England. This uncle was a lonely man;
his wife and nine children had died; his son Samuel had come
to Boston and opened a cutlery shop. Young Ben was the only
one of the family who bothered to read and reply to Uncle Benjamin's long letters of rhymes and ballads, prose tales and acros-
tics (verses in which the first letter of each line, read downward,
spelled a word) .

Ben's favorite was the acrostic on his own name which began,

> "B e to thy parents an obedient son
> E ach day let duty constantly be done
> N ever give way to sloth or lust or pride . . ."

and on through all the letters of his name.

This correspondence with his young nephew so fascinated
Uncle Benjamin that he sold his business in England and sailed
for Boston. For a time he lived with his brother Josiah, and
home life was even more interesting than before.

Months passed. The day of Ben's twelfth birthday came,
January 6 (by the old English calendar) , 1718. Mrs. Franklin
laid out a new shirt for her son and watched proudly as he put
it on.

"You're like my father, Ben," she said, pleased with the
thought. "Peter Folger of Nantucket was a fine man. His face
was like yours, Son, squarish; his shoulders broad; his fingers

long and skilled. He liked to read, too. I hope you will be a credit to him."

"I shall try, Mother," Ben said, impressed. His mother was not given to much talk.

"We must decide on your trade soon, Ben," Josiah remarked that evening. "You are twelve; it is time you were settled."

Not a word was said about the sea.

Some time later when the heavy snow had worn thin, the selection of Ben's trade came up again.

"The stock of candles is good," Josiah remarked at breakfast. "We can take today to show you different trades. We'll set out soon." He turned to his brother to explain. "I promised Ben that when he was twelve he could make a choice—you still don't like candlemaking, Son?"

"I should like to see other trades before I decide, Father," Ben said, shrewdly. He didn't intend to give up this day promised for seeing sights.

"Then make yourself neat, Ben," Josiah said. "We'll leave soon."

Ben scrubbed his hands and face and combed his hair. He put on his Sunday pants and coat, now getting tight, but still wearable. And his shirt was new; he did not need to button the coat all the way. His best shoes, hand-me-downs, of course, were clean. He brushed his tricorn hat and presented himself to his father.

"Very good, Son. You can look neat when you try. Now we'll go."

Their first visit was at a carpenter's shop. Ben liked the

scent of fresh shavings. He was fascinated as the apprentice planed a new board and the curls of wood dropped to the floor. The master shaped a table leg with his adz while two new apprentices whittled wooden pegs to hold the table together. It was a busy, pleasant place; Ben watched the workmen and stored up in his mind the way they got tasks done. But he did not suggest stopping their visits.

"The blacksmith's shop comes next," Josiah Franklin said. He had planned their tour carefully.

This shop was on Milk Street, not far from the house where Ben was born. He often passed by, too, when he delivered candles or soap, so it was no surprise. Two horses were being shod. The fire glowed as an apprentice pumped the bellows. The lad's face was red and sweaty. This would be no better than candles, certainly not in summer. Ben turned away.

At the tanner's, hides were drying on the wall; the smell did not encourage Ben to linger. The shoemaker did not interest him. Even Josiah, worried by this time, could not picture restless Ben sitting all day long on a bench, tapping pegs in the soles of shoes.

"We have wasted the better part of a day, my son," he said as they walked toward home. "Have you seen nothing you like?"

"I still like the sea, Father," Ben said cheerfully.

"Oh, the sea." Josiah sighed.

"You did not go to see Samuel?" Uncle Ben asked, when young Ben told of their visits.

"No," Josiah said. "You told me that Sam had a new apprentice only a month ago . . ."

"But he is doing so well," Uncle Ben said proudly. "Better see him."

The cutlery shop was tidy and clean. Two apprentices were busy at the back, and Sam was waiting on a customer. When he was free, Josiah explained their reason for coming.

"Well, I could take him." Sam gave Ben a critical inspection. "But you would have to pay me two pounds. He doesn't know much and may not be worth teaching."

"Pay!" Josiah was shocked. "No one else has asked for pay. Ben will make you a good apprentice."

"But you have to pay," Sam insisted.

"That I cannot, and will not, either." Josiah was vexed. "Sam's head is turned half way around," he complained as they left. "Because he is doing so well, he thinks everyone is rich."

The walk home was silent. As they came in the door, Mrs. Franklin could see by their faces that the visit had not been good. She spoke quickly, to make a diversion.

"And did you call and see your son James?" she asked.

"James?" Her husband stared at her. "And he just from London? What need would James have of an apprentice?"

"Oh, may we, Father?" Ben's eyes brightened. "I've not seen James in his shop."

"Well," Franklin was doubtful, and weary, too. "But if you like, Ben, we might as well go now." As they walked down the street, Franklin noticed that Ben was fresh as morning. Maybe the day will yet turn out something, he thought. Josiah Franklin was a hopeful man.

Ben Learns a Trade

It was not surprising that Josiah had omitted Ben's older brother James as a possible employer. Twenty-year-old James had recently come home after a year spent in London. There he had learned the printer's trade and had worked hard for money to buy a press and type. Opening a shop of his own in Boston was quite a venture; he had not yet proved that he could earn a living for himself—what need would he have for an apprentice?

Boston was then a town of about 10,000; it had many churches, ten bookstores, and several print shops. None of the printers was making a good living. Books came from London. Only sermons or advertisements for runaway servants or apprentices were printed locally. James announced that he could "print clear patterns on silk or calico without an offensive smell." But he got very little business.

However, Josiah thought as he and Ben walked toward the shop, we can try. I do not like this talk of the sea.

If you would not be forgotten . . .
write things worth reading
or do things worth the writing.

James eyed his brother thoughtfully. Having an apprentice to run errands would give an air to the shop. And he knew that Ben was a good reader—that might be useful.

"I'll take him, Father. But Ben will have to sign apprentice papers—no favoritism just because he is my brother."

"And you, Ben." Josiah longed to be fair. "Are you pleased?"

"You know I hanker for the sea, Father." Ben saw that dream was hopeless. "But ink is better than tallow. I'll go with James."

Papers were made out quickly before Ben could change his mind. He signed, promising to serve his brother until he was twenty-one (almost nine years) without pay until the last year; to be loyal; to keep shop secrets; and to obey. James, for his part, promised to furnish food and lodging and to teach Ben the printer's trade. James boarded near his shop, but was to be married and have his home soon. Josiah knew of this plan.

"Ben can sleep in the attic over the shop," James said. "I'll board him across the way; other apprentices eat there. It's handy. You run home and get your things, Ben. Then you will be here to start work in the morning."

Ben ran ahead of his father to tell his mother the news and to gather up his few clothes and books.

Work began early the next day. Ben's first task was washing type—soapy business. But in the afternoon James handed him a composer's stick and gave him a lesson in setting type. Almost at once Ben discovered that he was going to like being a printer. His fingers were long and dextrous; he did not fumble or spill type from the fonts. He was a good speller, too. James set him a task and turned away to his own work.

Eating with other apprentices was a new experience. The Franklin home had ever been cheerful and all the family busy. Here the boys quarreled loudly and seemed to have nothing to do, evenings. Ben learned that two of the boys worked in a bookshop.

"Oh, that must be wonderful!" Ben exclaimed fervently.

"Wonderful! Why?" They stared at him.

"Aren't you allowed to read the books?" Ben asked.

"Allowed! Who wants to read a book?"

"I do," Ben said. "I'd like to read every book in your shop."

"All at once?" The boys were dumbfounded.

"No, one at a time," Ben grinned.

"I'll bring you a book tonight," one boy said. "But I'll have to take it back in the morning—clean, too, mind you."

Now Ben was thankful that he had a tiny room by himself. He began a search for candle-ends—in gutters, shops, the boarding house. He read half the nights. He taught himself to read rapidly, getting the meaning of a paragraph at a glance so that the book could be returned in the morning.

One day a stranger came to the shop to have an advertisement printed. Having no work, Ben was crouched behind the press, reading.

"You like to read?" the stranger asked, surprised.

"Yes, sir, very much." Ben scrambled to his feet, politely.

"You're the first apprentice I ever heard of who likes to read. Tell your brother to send you with a proof of this copy. Then you may borrow a book and return it when you've read it."

Soon after this, Ben chanced to meet John Collins. John liked to read, and the two exchanged books and wrote each other comments on what they read. Ben found that this made him decide what he liked and didn't like about a book. He wished he had books of his own so he could look back and see again what he had read. One book John loaned him, *A Way to Health,* gave him an idea.

He chose his time carefully, when James had bowed out a customer.

"Would you like to save some money?" he asked casually.

"Of course. Who wouldn't?" retorted James.

"Give me *half* the money you pay for my board. You keep the other half. I'll board myself."

James scowled. Was there a catch to this?

"No trick," Ben said. "Just sense. You save half. I eat what I please."

"Done!" James said. He counted out the money for a week's board—shoved half to Ben, pocketed the rest. "Now there'll be no more fussing at table about underdone meat."

"I'll not even come to the table," Ben promised. That evening, after the shop closed, Ben went to market and bought hard biscuits, raisins, and rice. Tomorrow he would dash home and borrow that little kettle his mother never used because it was too small for her family. Then he'd cook rice and maybe, next week, get some potatoes. He bought no meat; the book approved a meatless diet. What he had bought should feed him for a week—and half the money James had given him was left over for buying books.

By the time he was fourteen years old, Ben had read many books; he was impressed by the works of Plato and Xenophon. He read about Socrates; this wise man thought that reason won more arguments than fighting. Ben tried mild ways with his brother and found that Socrates was right. This gave Ben a new idea; he had read for entertainment—now he saw that the right books might help him in his daily life.

Spurred by this discovery, he read Cotton Mather's book, *Essays to do Good,* and *Essays on Projects,* by Daniel Defoe. A project, Defoe explained, was a big undertaking that was needed but seemed almost impossible, such as Noah's Ark, in its day, or the Tower of Babel. One essay contained ideas for banks—Josiah's friends would have been astonished to know that Defoe thought well of banks; believed they helped a city grow. As he read, Ben's head whirled with the rush of new ideas Defoe gave him—about highways, insurance for houses—like insurance for ships—benevolent societies to help people in time of disaster. He read the whole book twice, straight through, making sure that he did not miss anything.

One day when Ben was sweeping out the shop, he noticed a small book—the third volume of the *Spectator,* by Joseph Addison. He showed it to James.

"Someone's left it," James said indifferently.

"May I read it?" Ben tried to pretend he didn't really care.

"If you like. But keep it clean. Someone may call for it."

That evening in his attic, Ben munched raisins and biscuits and read the book several times. He enjoyed the smooth
sentences as well as the interesting ideas.

I could write like that, Ben told himself.

James was married, now, and had a baby daughter; he often
stayed at home awhile at noon. So, the day after Ben discovered
Addison, he sharpened a quill pen, and as soon as James left,
wrote the essay from memory. In the evening he compared his

writing with Addison's. Alas! His memory was *too* good. What he had written was almost exactly Addison's words; there was nothing to correct.

I'll wait awhile. I'll read something else, Ben thought. Then I shall write it again. This is my project. So a few days later Ben cut his written copy into sentences, shook the bits of paper in a hat, and then tried to fit them together correctly. When he compared this with the printed essay, he was much pleased; most of it was as Addison wrote it. But some parts, he thought, were improved by his changes. He was vastly encouraged about writing.

A chance remark soon after this reminded Ben of the verses he and Uncle Benjamin used to write to each other. There had been a tragic drowning in the Bay; Ben wrote the story of it in verse—it was very sad. He called the long poem *The Lighthouse Tragedy*.

"Those verses are good," James said. "We might print them and sell them on the street." By "we" he meant Ben. The apprentice went at the work, pleased with James's approval.

The ballad sold quickly, and James made a neat profit. But his father was annoyed, and came to the shop to object.

"Ben is apprenticed to learn the printer's trade, not to write drivel. I had trouble enough when he was younger and wrote such stuff to his uncle. He can never earn a living writing poetry. He should stick to printing." Josiah felt so strongly that James had to agree. So Ben continued to work hard in the shop six days a week and to read Sundays, nights, and at odd hours.

Time seemed to pass quickly. It was autumn of 1719 when James hurried into the shop with news.

"I'm hired to print a newspaper," he cried to Ben and two friends who were loafing in the shop.

"Boston's got a newspaper," one friend said. *The News-Letter.* Why have another one?"

"This new paper will be better. It's to be called the *Gazette.* I'm getting new type, and I'll rearrange my shop—this is the chance I've been hoping for!" He set Ben to work at once, cleaning and sorting type. "Then clean the fonts and this room. We'll start work tomorrow."

James Franklin's shop printed forty numbers of the *Gazette;* then the postmaster at Boston was changed, and James lost his contract. A postmaster could easily have a newspaper delivered; so, for a long time in colonial America, postmasters owned the newspapers and had them printed on contract. The postmaster general, in London, could change postmasters when he pleased.

James Franklin brooded over his disappointment. He had spent money in this venture; his pride was hurt, too, even more than his pocketbook.

Suddenly, in his gloom, a daring idea popped into his head. "I'll have a newspaper of my own!" he said. He got up and stamped around the shoproom. "What was that *Gazette*— a little 7 by 11 sheet with warmed-over news from London, four months old."

Ben stared at his brother—and an idea came into *his* head. "Who'll write your news?" he asked, his heart pounding.

"Oh, friends of mine; I know several who can write. I'll call my paper the *New England Courant*—after the London paper. I'll print news of our own town.

"There'll be no trouble with postmasters, because you will deliver it yourself, Ben. After you print it."

Ben's eagerness died. Still, James's plan was something new. If he bided his time, even an apprentice might write.

The friends James counted on were young men who had a habit of dropping in to the shop for talk. They were pleased with his idea for a newspaper.

"It'll be a sensation!"

"We'll hunt news for you that will startle readers."

"Better have a care though," warned one. "You might be arrested if you displease anyone in the church or in the government."

The first issue of the paper was dated August 17, 1721. It was neatly printed in clear type on good paper. In addition to the moon and tide and ship news for the week, readers found many newsy bits about Boston people and events—some sure to bring a laugh.

"They liked it, Brother!" Ben reported when he returned from delivery. Every paper sold.

Now the writers gathered every morning and discussed what should go into the next issue. They quickly learned that it is easy to arouse people to be *against* something. They called themselves radicals and thought up causes they could oppose.

That summer Boston was suffering a terrible epidemic of smallpox. Three years earlier, the idea of inoculation had been brought to America from Turkey, and Increase Mather and his son Cotton, both ministers in Boston, were trying to get people to be inoculated. James and his friends knew nothing about medicine, but they picked inoculation as a timely topic and wrote against it.

People could hardly wait till the next issue of the *Courant* got on the streets to see what arguments the paper had printed.

The young radicals couldn't have found a better subject to make talk; every reader had opinions, and few had knowledge.

Smallpox ended when winter came, but by then the young men had no trouble finding other topics to interest readers. James prospered and drove his young brother to harder and harder work. The brothers quarreled often; James sometimes struck his apprentice. Ben forgot the advice of Socrates and was often angry.

He couldn't get that paper out except for me, Ben brooded in his room at night. I mean to write for it, not merely print it. James wouldn't print my work—never mind. I'll outwit him!

A few mornings later, as James entered the shop, he found a sheaf of folded papers slipped under the front door. Ben watched him pick them up, read a page or two, smiling.

"We have a contributor," James said to the radicals as they drifted in, soon. "Read it, and see what you think."

Ben, scrubbing type, watched as the papers were read.

"Silence Dogood; a minister's widow," one said. "No female could write as well as this!"

"No *man* would claim to be a female!" another exclaimed.

"This is good for the paper—shall we take it?" James asked. The others agreed; so Ben set it up.

Silence Dogood's tale was chatty, unlike anything Boston readers had seen. It broke off skillfully, promising more in "my next letter." The papers sold out in an hour.

Ben did not disappoint his readers; every other week papers were found under the door, each more daring than the last. Harvard College, the ministers, the Lord Brethren, and plainer folk alike came in for spoofing. People grabbed each paper, wondering whose turn was next.

The day came when Ben, flushed with success, confessed his secret. The radicals lauded him. James gave him a beating, which Ben felt was totally undeserved—wasn't the paper succeeding? Ben was bitter, but he continued writing until he had done fourteen numbers.

By then the radicals, taught by Ben's example, did not miss him. They wrote daring articles themselves—but they were not as skillful; one article offended a member of the Boston Assembly, and James, the publisher, was thrown into prison.

Ben, the apprentice, was called into court, but told nothing. James, loyal as all Franklins were, would not expose his friends, so he served out his sentence of one month.

Furious at this indignity to a Franklin, Ben wrote an intemperate article against injustice that brought a court command; James was to stop publishing the *Courant*. Mr. Franklin, the radicals, and James, just released, held a hasty conference.

"We'd better issue under a new name," one suggested.

"They'd see through that. Stop the paper for a time."

"That's too bad when it is selling so well," Franklin said.

"Let Ben be publisher. He does the work." The brothers flushed—Ben at the praise, James with anger.

"But he's only an apprentice."

"Why don't you cancel his papers, James," a friend said, "just in case the magistrate asks. Then we could go on as now."

James could think of nothing better, so he cancelled the

apprentice papers. But he whispered to Ben, "This changes nothing—hear me!" Ben understood what James meant when his brother had him sign new, secret indenture papers. But he thrilled when he saw his name as publisher in the next issue!

Ben worked harder than ever. He studied each piece he wrote, making sure it had nothing to offend. The *Courant* prospered, but James's temper grew worse. Ben decided to get another job, but though he made the rounds of print shops, he found no work. James had seen to that.

One night Ben lay awake thinking what to do. Blows were more frequent; the shop, however successful, was no longer a good place. The sea? Ben wondered. No, he had outgrown that longing. He'd rather be a printer. Surely there are print shops in New York; he'd heard the name of one printer, William Bradford. Suddenly he had decided. He would go to New York and find a job.

John Collins helped him get away. John sold some of Ben's precious books and bought a passage. John helped him carry his things to the Long Wharf and board ship. John kept the secret until after the turn of tide in the morning, when he saw the ship, bending under a good breeze, sail down the Bay.

On board, Ben Franklin, seventeen years old, watched Boston and all he had known fade into the morning mist. He had learned a trade he liked; he had proved that he could write— and now he was escaping four more years of apprenticeship. Ben felt fine.

Ben Comes to Philadelphia

New York was a small town of less than 8,000 people that autumn day of 1723 when Ben Franklin left the ship and jauntily set out to find William Bradford. He saw houses set close together, their odd gables turned toward the narrow, twisting streets. He noticed the well-scrubbed walks and doorstones and the gleaming window panes. His mother would admire those.

By watching signs, he soon found the Bradford print shop and pounded on the shining brass knocker. When the door opened, he introduced himself and told his reason for calling.

"So you want a job, lad," Bradford said. "Come in." He closed the door and gestured toward a three-legged stool. Sitting opposite, he folded his leather apron back, cornerwise, and thoughtfully studied Ben's face.

"You must think New York is Philadelphia," he remarked. "Now *that* city has the printing business! But I couldn't abide

Approve not him
who commends all you say.

the Governor of Pennsylvania, so I left. My son Andrew might
have hired you if you were there—but you are here." He
chuckled. Ben tried to smile, but the news was disappointing.

"This town is Dutch," Bradford went on, "so not a good
place for an English printer. New York's not a reading town,
either, so I don't carry books. And I don't know Dutch."

"Maybe, if I went to Philadelphia," Ben began.

"Maybe. I make no promise. Andrew's best printer died,
but you are young and . . ."

"A good printer," Ben added, with an engaging smile. "I
set and printed the *New England Courant;* I did all of it when
my brother had, well, other business." A prison sentence, himself a runaway, were not good topics to bring up.

"Philadelphia is a long way from here, but if you go," Bradford said, "tell Andrew I sent you." The instructions he gave
for the journey were certainly not encouraging.

As Ben walked back toward the wharves a sudden breeze
brought a whiff of salt air that made him stop and think. Now,
today, he had a chance to go to sea—no job, no ties, many ships
along this wharf where a strong lad could surely get a job. He
paused—but only for a moment. Once the sea had meant freedom. Now he had freedom and also a trade he enjoyed. Nearby
he saw a small boat rocking as waves lapped the piles. Perhaps
this boat . . .

"I'm for Philadelphia," he called, walking toward it.

"You haven't looked well at my boat," the sailor said un-
happily. "I'd never make it around to the Delaware River by
sea. But I could ferry you over to Amboy."

"Would I get a stage there?" Bradford had not mentioned a stage.

The sailor roared. "There is no stage. At Amboy you start walking fifty miles to Burlington—less you have a horse, Mister."

"I'd like to walk," Ben said, relieved about the cost. "Wait for me. I must tell the Boston captain to send my chest around by sea." He dashed off. In the hold of the ship that had brought him from Boston, he opened his chest, took out a shirt, some socks, and a few other small things. He stuffed these in his pockets, re-locked his chest, found the captain, and paid its transport to Philadelphia. That ship would not leave till it got a cargo—days, maybe weeks, hence. Then he hurried back to the small boat. Two other passengers had come, and they set sail for Amboy.

But alas, as they rounded the tip of Manhattan Island, the gentle breeze turned into a storm that blew them off their course. The sails were torn to shreds, and the boat was all but sunk. Thirty hours later, Ben landed at Amboy, weary, wet, and hungry, to begin his fifty-mile walk to Burlington on the Delaware.

An autumn rain that lasted all the days of his journey kept Ben chilled. He was hungry, too, but he did not think of giving up, not even when he got to Burlington and found he had just missed the boat to Philadelphia. By offering to row, he wangled a seat in a small craft that was leaving soon, and the next morning he was at his destination.

In New York Ben had liked his appearance. Now, as he climbed to the wharf, he looked at his clothes and was dismayed. His three-cornered hat drooped; his coat was muddy, and the pockets, stuffed with his things, sagged wetly. His shoes were mud-caked, and his stomach ached with hunger.

Soberly he counted his money—a silver Dutch dollar and some coppers. With a grand gesture he paid the boatman, though he had rowed all night as he had bargained.

Silly! he thought. Because I am poor, I try to act rich. But the money was gone. He climbed the river bank and walked up a wide, quiet street. Market stalls in the center of the street were closed, reminding Ben that this was Sunday—would a bake shop be open? Down a way he spied a boy carrying loaves of bread. He ran toward him. "Sell me a loaf, please!" he called.

"Can't sell these, they're bought; I'm delivering them." Ben looked so disappointed that the lad added, "Go to the back door of that shop—see? They'll sell you something."

In the shop Ben bought three pennies' worth of "rolls" and to his amazement got, not rolls as in Boston, but what he would call loaves of bread. "Is this right?" he asked, putting down his money.

"You must be a stranger to wonder at the price," the youth laughed. "Farmers bring in wheat; bread is cheap here, and good."

Smiling, Ben thrust a loaf under each arm and walked out, munching hungrily at the third. The bread *was* good. Already his stomach felt better, so he strolled on. As he neared the fourth cross street, he saw a pretty girl, about his own age, standing on a doorstep. She laughed when she saw him. Ben, knowing how ridiculous he must look, laughed back.

Suddenly he was thirsty. The pretty girl had gone inside,

so he hurried back to the river, and kneeling, drank his fill. A woman and child, passengers on the boat he had come on, were still there. In a generous mood, he gave away his two loaves, then turned and went back up the street.

By this time some Quakers—he knew them by their dress—were walking to their meeting house. Ben followed them, sat in a back pew, and in the quiet of Quaker meeting went sound asleep.

He wakened with a start as a kindly voice asked, "Does thee

want to go home now?" Home! Ben had no place to lay his head.

"If you could direct me to a lodging house, sir," Ben said, "respectable, but very cheap?"

The Quaker smiled and led Ben to a corner from which he pointed out a brick house. Ben found that he had pennies enough to sleep there, but nothing left over for breakfast. In his tiny room, he pulled off the wet clothes and spread them on the chair. He put his hat on the floor, careful to pat it into shape. Then he lay down and slept for hours—slept till wakened by Monday's sun.

He got up quickly, washed well, tidied his clothes as best he could, and set out to find the Bradford print shop. To his astonishment, William Bradford of New York opened the door.

"I didn't expect to see you here, sir!" Ben exclaimed.

"I came a-horseback. It's faster than footing it, Ben. I told my son about you, but he had already filled the job; you know I made you no promise."

"Oh, I know, sir." Ben's face must have shown his bitter disappointment, because Bradford's tone became more cordial.

"Come right in," he invited. "We're eating breakfast, and there's plenty for you. While we eat, we'll think of something."

As Ben ate bread and kippers piled on his plate, the younger Bradford got an idea.

"Samuel Keimer might hire Ben," he said. Then he turned to explain to his father. "Keimer's newly come to town. I hear he means to open a print shop and bookstore. Likely he'd want an experienced hand to help. I'll take Ben right over."

"No, I'll take him myself." Bradford pushed his empty plate aside, got his hat, and opened the door.

"You may come back here, Ben. There's plenty of room for you to sleep in the attic till you get a start," Andrew called as they left.

Keimer liked Ben. "Let me see you handle the stick," he said.

Ben went to the press; it was dirty and needed repair. The fonts were broken, and the type filthy, but he did the best he could as he set up two sentences, which Keimer hardly noticed.

The newcomer was telling Bradford his plans. Ben felt sure he did not know Bradford was a printer; for if he knew, he would not talk so freely.

"The boy can work for me until he cleans the press and type," Keimer ended. "When my plans work out, I'll hire him regular."

Bradford looked pleased, almost smug, as he turned to leave.

Ben worked for three days repairing that press; Keimer didn't know how to operate it, though he had brought it from France. The type was English, but there was so little that only part of a job could be set up at a time. After that, Ben did a small job for Andrew Bradford.

A few days later Keimer sent for Ben.

"I hear you've been staying in a printer's family. You're hired out to me now, and I'll get you a place to stay, too. I don't want you mixed up with another shop." He took Ben to a house on Market Street; introduced him to Mrs. Read, who accepted

him as a boarder. Ben was glad to have a place to live, for he had word that his chest had come. He went to the ship, got it from the hold, and, poising it on his shoulder, carried it to the Read home.

"This is my daughter Deborah," Mrs. Read said when he returned.

Ben grinned, and the pretty girl laughed—a nice laugh.

"So you are the youth with the loaves!" Mrs. Read laughed

too. Ben nodded and carried his chest up the stairs.

A new life now began for Benjamin Franklin. Keimer paid good wages. The Read home was pleasant; meals were excellent, and in the evenings he enjoyed music, games, and talk with Deborah and her young friends. Ben often thanked his good fortune that brought him to Philadelphia.

And well might he be thankful! William Penn's colony was prosperous and kind to strangers. Quakers, unlike the religious folk of Boston, were tolerant; they allowed a person to think and to worship in his own way. Because of this freedom, Germans and Swiss, as well as English people, came there, settling in town or back in the forests where they soon developed prosperous farms. Ben was pleased with all he heard and saw of the place and people.

Some evenings he spent in Keimer's shop with three young men who became special friends. Joseph Watson liked to talk religion; Charles Osborne would debate any topic; and James Ralph, Ben's favorite, was a poet. Ben thrived on all these advantages.

Into this delightful world came a letter from Captain Holmes of Newcastle, a town some forty miles down the river. Holmes was married to one of Ben's older sisters; he had just returned from a voyage to Boston where he learned of Ben's leaving home.

"You should return home at once (he wrote) ; your family are much concerned about you."

"Go back! Never!" Ben said the words aloud as the letter dropped to the table. But as he picked it up and read again, he saw that Holmes meant well; since he was a brother-in-law, he deserved a polite reply. Ben wrote a carefully composed letter, giving his reasons for his decision to stay where he was.

This letter was handed to Captain Holmes by a sailor to whom Ben had entrusted it in Philadelphia. At the moment of receiving it, the captain chanced to be talking with Governor Keith about a shipping matter. He begged pardon and hastily glanced at the letter.

"My young brother-in-law likes Philadelphia," he remarked to the governor. "He is a printer, and he intends to stay."

"We need printers," Keith said, kindly. "Could I help him?"

"He seems well set up," Holmes smiled. "But read the letter, sir."

"A bright lad—seventeen, do I understand?" Keith remarked as he read. "I'll get in touch with him." He returned the letter, and they finished their business. Holmes thought no more of the matter, but Keith remembered.

Sir William Keith had been in the colony since 1716, first as customs officer, later appointed by the Penns as governor. The province of Pennsylvania had the usual colonial form of government, an assembly, elected by the people, and a governor, appointed in England, who had power to veto anything the assembly did. Keith was liked by many; his record with the Indians was perhaps the best in the new world. But he was undependable in personal matters—Bradford had suffered through him; hence his remark in New York.

Soon after Ben had written to Captain Holmes, he was

setting type in the shop when Keimer, at the window, spied
two gentlemen about to knock at his door.

"It's the governor!" Keimer cried. "Now we'll get new
work!" He tossed away his leather apron and dashed down
the stairs.

"You have a young printer here? One Ben Franklin?"
Keimer was so astonished he could hardly say, "Yes, sir!"

"Call him, please. I need talk with him." Ben hurried
down, and the governor introduced himself. "We will talk at
the inn," he said.

Ben was astonished, and Keimer didn't know whether to
be offended at being left out or pleased that his shop was noticed.

"I have heard of you from your brother-in-law, Captain
Holmes," Keith began when they had ordered. "I want you
to open your own shop."

"But I have no money, sir. It would take a hundred
pounds!"

"Your father will loan it to you, Ben. I'll write a letter
that will turn the trick. He cannot refuse a governor. I've
engaged passage to Boston. You are to go in two days—and
good luck follow you!"

Ben was amazed, but he dared not dispute a governor. So
it was that in the spring of 1724, when he was eighteen, Ben
sailed for Boston. He had used his two days to buy new clothes,
shoes, and a gold watch and chain. He intended to make his
return with a dash.

His very real pleasure on seeing his family surprised him,
though he had missed them, especially Jane, his youngest sister.

"Now you will stay," his mother said happily.

"Well, no, Mother, that is not the plan." He handed his father the governor's letter.

Josiah Franklin read the letter twice, folded it, and handed it to Ben. "I'm glad the governor takes to you, Ben. But he forgets that you are a youth, only eighteen. I do not have a hundred pounds to venture, Son. Thank the governor and tell him that if he is of the same mind when you are twenty-one, perhaps we may talk again."

"But you'll stay, Ben?" Jane begged.

Ben shook his head. "I like Philadelphia. I make good wages. I have friends. I don't blame you, Father. I'll make the governor understand."

Benjamin stayed on a few days, though. He visited James's shop and annoyed that brother with his airs. A runaway apprentice with new clothes and a gold watch was too much. Ben did not make the visit easy; James seemed to rouse Ben's very worst side. Ben was not asked to see James's wife and children.

But on the whole the visit was a happy one.

Ben sailed for New York on a sloop that put in at Newport, so he went ashore and called on his beloved brother John. While he was there, Mr. Vernon, a neighbor, came to ask a favor.

"I hear you live in Pennsylvania," he said. "A man there owes me money. Will you please collect it? Later I can plan to get it from you some way." The request did not surprise Ben. People did not travel much, and exchange of money was a real difficulty. Mr. Vernon gave him an order to collect the debt, and Ben promised to do so.

When the sloop got to New York, Ben was astonished to see John Collins awaiting him on the wharf. Collins had been fascinated by tales of Ben's success and had taken a fast ship to join him as his uninvited guest. On the way to Philadelphia, Ben collected Mr. Vernon's money and secreted it carefully. But Collins' expenses were so heavy that before he realized what he was doing, Ben had spent some—an act of wrongdoing that weighed on his conscience even as he used the cash.

My father is right, Ben thought. I am not to be trusted.

Fortunately, Keimer welcomed Ben, and hard work with good wages began at once. At first Ben's friends liked John Collins, but when he did not find work, they liked him less—Philadelphians expected to work hard. Ben was relieved when Collins sailed away to Barbadoes; he resolved to pay back the borrowed money as soon as possible.

Governor Keith was undaunted by Josiah Franklin's refusal.

"Never mind, Ben," he said cheerfully. "Make out a list of what you want, and I'll send to London for it. I'm determined that you shall do my government printing in your own shop.

"Wait a minute! I have a better idea. Make out that list and *take* it to London!" Men around him gasped in a way Keith enjoyed. "I count on you, Ben. Stay long enough to learn smart new fashions in type. See the newest books and pamphlets. I mean to have this colony keep up with London. It's my big ambition!"

Ben, his head whirling, began his list.

A Stranger in London

Those lists were made and remade many times as weeks of summer passed. Ben saw the governor frequently.

"Better engage your passage, Ben," Keith always advised. "I'll have those letters ready soon." But he didn't mention money—and passage to London cost ten pounds.

I guess the governor depends on me for details, Ben thought, and did not know whether to be worried or pleased. He paid passage on the *London Hope,* a ship that was to sail in the autumn. He arranged with Keimer for leave and had an "understanding" with Deborah Read that they would be married when he returned. Still no letters!

Then one day he met the governor on the street.

"I hear the *London Hope* is sailing tomorrow," Keith said. "I've been so rushed—but you may count on getting those letters on board when the ship stops at Newcastle. I'm on my way there now."

Look before, or you'll
find yourself behind.

The governor's manner was so cordial that Ben's doubts vanished. He ran to tell Keimer he was leaving. He dashed to the Reads' to finish packing and to tell Deborah good-by. Then he boarded ship.

To his astonishment, James Ralph was sitting on the deck.

"Surprised you, eh?" Ralph laughed. "I told you I was going, too, but you didn't believe me!"

"Well, you do have a wife and child," Ben said. He had thought that his friend, being older, was settled. "But I shall enjoy your company," he added truthfully.

At Newcastle Colonel French came aboard, and, with quite an air, gave the captain a pouch of mail—"from the governor," he said. "Yours are in there," he told Ben, and wished him luck.

At the last minute word came that two cabin passengers they awaited could not sail. This left the best cabin empty. The captain had noticed Colonel French's chat with Franklin, so he moved Ben and his friend into these good quarters.

"Oh, thank you, Captain!" Ben could hardly believe his good fortune. "And now may I have my letters from the governor?"

"Letters? I have no time for letters now! You'll get them before we dock at London." The captain shouted sailing orders.

The voyage, begun that bright November day, was long; the weather was cold and stormy. Ben was thankful for a cheerful cabin; he enjoyed Ralph's company and made a friend of Thomas Denham, a Quaker merchant bound for London to buy merchandise for a store. But for worry about those letters, he would have been happy.

When they were in the English Channel, the captain opened the mail pouch. "There was nothing for you, Franklin," he reported.

"Nothing?" Ben cried out. "But the governor said . . ."

"Oh, there are a few letters from the governor. Look them over." He handed Ben five. "Are these what you expected?"

Ben looked at each one. "The governor has mentioned these names to me," he said. "One is to a printer."

"Likely he meant you to deliver them," the captain said.

As soon as the ship tied up, Ben and his friend hurried ashore and found a cheap boarding house. Then Ben went to deliver the letters. He watched anxiously as the first man opened his envelope.

"This letter is not from the governor," the man exclaimed. "It's from a rascal of a lawyer, trying to collect a bill I have paid." He threw it down and turned to a customer.

Ben wandered down the street, too shocked to think clearly. Would a *governor* be so deceitful? What should a youth do in this big, strange city? Suddenly the name of Thomas Denham came to his mind. The Quaker had mentioned the inn where he would stop; Ben hurried to the place.

Denham was there; he listened gravely to Ben's tale.

"Didn't you know Keith's character?" he asked, surprised.

"He's the governor. I trusted him, sir."

"So has the Penn family—thus far," Denham admitted. "Oh, Keith has many fine qualities; few men are all bad, Ben. But Keith likes to manage destinies; he has more imagination than good sense. As for credit—he is deeply in debt here and at home. You couldn't buy a press for him without cash. Let's see your other letters." He opened them. Each contained a blank piece of paper.

"What shall I do, sir?" Ben felt himself shaking.

"You know a trade that is respected in London," Denham said kindly. "Get a job. Save money for passage home. Meanwhile, as you work, see London. This may prove to be a great opportunity for you."

Ben's spirits soared. He thanked his good friend and hurried to tell James Ralph the news.

"Well, here we are," Ralph said, taking Ben's disappointment easily. "You have funds; I'll soon have a good job on the stage. I'm set on that."

Ben counted his cash. Fifteen Spanish pistoles (about twelve English pounds) and a few other coins. "With yours this will last us for a while," he said.

"Oh, I have nothing, not a shilling," James said airily. "I spent my all for passage. But I shall soon be rich. Meanwhile, there are print shops." They went out and got a good meal (Ben paid), and Ben got a job at Palmer's, a large print shop Ben knew of from Keimer. He was to start work at once and get thirty shillings a week, the best wages he had ever earned.

Months went by. Ralph got no work; he sold no prose or verse. Instead, he "borrowed" from Ben until the fifteen pistoles were gone, then shared Ben's wages. He was an agreeable companion; he made many friends—while Ben was working. Evenings were a gay whirl—music, theater, and talk with these companions.

In his daily work, Ben learned a great deal about printing, though he did not overwork. He enjoyed himself and drifted. He wrote to Deborah that he liked London; he might never return to Philadelphia; and he suggested ending their "understanding."

But gradually James Ralph became an intolerable burden. The two quarreled bitterly. Ralph left London without a good-by.

In an effort to start anew, Ben quit Palmer's and got a job at Watts's—a larger shop, where he earned better wages. He moved to another boarding house and began to save his money. Two happenings at Watts's helped him in this time of change.

Ben did not drink beer; the other workmen did.

"You have to drink to get strong, Ben," one told him.

"Water-American!" they called him, teasing. Ben laughed with good humor—but did not change his ways. The next day, in a hurry, he picked up two heavy cases and carried them up the stairs! The men stopped work to gape at him—*they* carried one case at a time! They continued to call him "Water-American," but the nickname was spoken with pride, not scorn. The other happening came more slowly; he made two new friends in the shop, David Hall and a young man named Wygate, who was well educated. One evening's talk with Wygate brought back Ben's love of books—how could he have gone so long without reading! Wygate knew of a circulating library where second-hand books could be rented cheaply. His evenings, now, were spent in reading and discussing, which he found he enjoyed more than James Ralph's gaiety.

This winter of 1726-7 was an important time for literature and science in London. Sir Isaac Newton, philosopher and mathematician, was making a stir with new ideas. Pope, Swift, Defoe, were in the city, writing. Wygate liked Defoe as Ben did; they talked for hours about his essays. Voltaire was coming to London, Ben heard, so they read his work.

Through Wygate, Ben had the good fortune to meet Sir Hans Sloane; he was making a collection of rare articles which became the start of the British Museum. Ben sold to Sir Hans a small purse made of asbestos that he had brought with him as a novelty. He also met Peter Collinson, a wealthy young man who was interested in science—Collinson called it natural philosophy.

As spring came, Wygate and Ben often walked along the Thames. One warm evening, Ben tossed off his coat and shoes and plunged into the river.

"You'll drown!" Wygate cried. Ben bobbed up, laughing.

"Not I!" He dived again and came up yards off, down river. When he saw that Wygate was really frightened, he swam near and explained.

"When I was a lad," he said, "we lived near a millpond. I learned to swim as easily as to walk."

"Teach me," Wygate begged. In two lessons Ben had his friend swimming—and found himself with a reputation that would have brought well-paid work teaching swimming, if he had cared for it.

But with the turn to books, Ben found his thoughts going back to Philadelphia. He was ashamed of the letter he had written to Deborah. He thought with longing of the friendly ways of Philadelphia. Did he want to stay in London always? What *did* he want?

Occasionally he had called on Mr. Denham, at the Quaker's invitation. Now he went to him for advice.

"What should I do with my life, sir?" he asked. "I have learned much that is new about printing. But I have not yet saved enough money for passage home. I have no plan—what ought I do?"

Denham saw Ben was earnest and disturbed.

"I think you should go to Philadelphia; you belong there. You are lost in London. And I can help you start a new life."

"New, sir? Not printing?"

"Not printing. You know I plan to open a store at home. I will hire you as my clerk, bookkeeper, and assistant. Start at once; I need help as I finish buying my stock. I will advance you passage money and pay you fifty pounds a year with more later as you get experience. I plan to do business in the West Indies; you can manage that—you could make a good thing of it, I promise you."

"I accept—and thank you, sir. Thank you very much."

Ben gave notice at Watts's, and then went to work for Mr. Denham. He felt a deep devotion to the Quaker; the man was like a father to him.

Soon goods were packed and aboard the ship *Berkshire;* on July 22, 1726, they sailed westward, for home.

Ben was twenty and a half years old, now, and his mood was very different from when he voyaged with James Ralph eighteen months earlier. His London experiences had matured him; he was interested in the ship and in nature; he had an urge to observe and to write down all he saw. He began a diary and entered the movements of the wind, which was not favorable on this voyage. At times it blew hard from the west, and the ship got off its course. Other days the wind vanished, and the ship rocked idly on a glassy sea. Ben recorded, too, an eclipse of the moon and a sudden almost total eclipse of the sun that surprised them one day.

But living creatures were even more interesting to watch: fish of many kinds, and birds—one circled the ship now and then and rested high in the rigging. Dolphins fascinated him, so gay and graceful that he watched them for hours. Often he dived over the ship's side to wash himself and his shirt. Once he spied a shark just in time to stop his plunge. He stood by the rail, watching the fierce creature and the pilot fish that surrounded him, wondering why they were not eaten. Afternoons he played draughts (checkers), a game he enjoyed because it made him think.

The voyage lasted about three months, and near the end

Ben began to study himself. Why had he lost two good friends, Collins and Ralph? Had he been wrong to let them depend on him? Why had he been so wasteful and foolish in London? Could he make himself a better man? Should this be his project? He got pad and pencil and in a sheltered corner of the deck began to write:

1. It is necessary for me to be frugal for some time.
2. To endeavor to speak the truth in every instance.
3. To apply myself to whatever business I take in hand.
4. I resolve to speak ill of no man.

There was more to be said about each point, but these four simple resolutions pleased him. Each morning he read them over and pondered. He had violated these ideals. The debt to Mr. Vernon troubled him especially. For the future he resolved to follow the pattern he had set down. Ben did not mention the paper to Mr. Denham. Let the good Quaker see by acts that Ben was making himself worthy of kindness.

On the 9th of October the glad cry, "Land! Land!" came from aloft. The next day a pilot boarded, bringing a peck of apples, which tasted wonderful after weeks of salted food. On the 11th they sailed up the Delaware and landed at Philadelphia.

Ben was astonished at the changes he soon discovered. Governor Keith had been dismissed, and a new governor had come. Ben passed the former governor on the street, and Keith turned away, flushing. Deborah's father had died. Mrs. Read, annoyed at Ben, had pushed Deborah into marriage with a Mr. Rogers,

a potter by trade. Along with this news, Ben heard more gossip:
Rogers already had a wife in England; he had gone to the West
Indies and died, leaving debts. Was Deborah a widow if she
had never been a wife?

Ben's good friend Watson had died; Osborne had moved
to the West Indies. Keimer prospered; he had a new print shop
with a fine stationery store on the first floor. There were scores
of changes.

Mr. Denham opened a store on Water Street and with
Ben's help displayed his merchandise attractively. Customers
came and bought. Ben studied nights, learning selling and
accounting. As January and his twenty-first birthday ap-
proached, life seemed full of goodness.

What sort of young man did his friends see as they looked at
the returned printer, now a merchant? Benjamin Franklin was
about five foot, ten inches tall, with the square look he always
had—chin and face above squarish shoulders. Gray eyes were
friendly; clothes plain and always spotless. His speech tended
to be slow; he wrote faster and better than he talked. His manner was gracious and sincere.

Ben was only recently beginning to show that he had many
sides to his nature: alertness for business and his advancement,
keenness in observing nature—his notes aboard ship were his
first evidence of that interest. He realized his good fortune in
returning to Philadelphia, and was for the first time conscious
of a feeling for the city, the colony, for America. He had vague
thoughts that perhaps one should do something to share in the
making of such a place. He was intelligent and maturing, a

coming important merchant, customers told each other.

Then, with a sudden turn of fate, everything changed.

Mr. Denham and Ben were taken ill the same day. Ben had acute pleurisy; the doctors could not name Denham's illness. Both were too ill to remember business. Ben could think of nothing except that when he died the pain would stop.

He was lying weak and suffering when he learned that his cherished friend had died. Ben thought dimly that surely the world would stop when that good Quaker left it.

"You are to stay on and get well," members of the Denham family told him. Though Mr. Denham was dead, Ben learned thas his kindness still reached out to him—the debt for passage money was cancelled, and Ben was left a small sum, enough to tide him through recovery and the transition into a new job. No one could carry on the new store. That was gone—and with it hopes of future advancement.

Ben thanked those who brought the news. Then he turned his face to the wall until he could control his emotion. A man of twenty-one should not weep. He should think and plan—but how could he, now?

One thing was clear; he must start over again, and the beginning would be at the bottom.

The Pennsylvania Gazette

Ben's strength returned slowly; he had far too much time to think of his uncertain future. Then a call from Captain Freeman of Boston made an interesting diversion for the convalescent.

"I just got in," the captain said, "and I promised your family that I would come at once and tell you about Jane. She is going to be married—a nice man, too, Edward Mecom."

"Jane!" Ben exclaimed. "She is only fifteen! But I thank you for the message."

"Well, she'll soon be a married woman. I'll be in port three-four days. If you want to send her a letter, I'll take it."

The thought that he was remembered seemed to give Ben new vigor. He would send a letter, of course—and a gift, too. He spent the rest of the day thinking what to buy for her. The next day, his twenty-first birthday, he bought a gift and wrote a letter. Then he took both to Captain Freeman.

The letter was tender and affectionate; she was his fa-

If you would keep
your secret from an enemy,
tell it not to a friend.

vorite sister, he wrote; he'd always known she would be a fine woman . . .

> I have been thinking what would be a suitable present . . .
> I had almost determined on a tea table but when I considered
> that the character of a good housewife was far preferable to that
> of being only a gentlewoman, I concluded to send you a spinning
> wheel which I hope you will accept as a small token of my sin-
> cere love and affection . . . I am, dear Jenny,
>
> Your loving brother, B. Franklin.

The generous gift reduced Ben's already low finances, but he knew Jane would be pleased. And before he had time to worry, Keimer sent for him to call at the shop when he was able. Ben presented himself two days later.

"I can't tend shop and store both," Keimer began complaining before Ben closed the door. "I'll run this store. You take charge of the printing upstairs. Go up and look it over. Come back, Ben; I'll pay good wages."

When Ben saw that shop, he knew the reason for the offer of work—the place was in dreadful condition! The floor was dirty, type scattered with rubbish; the press was broken; several men and boys stood about, loafing. Ben, with his love of neatness and order, felt a surge of vigor. I'm needed here! he thought, happily.

"I'll take over," he called down the stairs.

In two hours the place was transformed. The floor was swept, the windows washed. The fonts were cleaned and broken type picked out, all while Ben worked on the broken press. The men liked the new boss because they saw he knew the business. He was courteous, too, and worked even harder than they did.

As days passed in the busy, orderly shop, Ben learned to know and, in the main, to like the men. Two had come from the "back country" expecting to make their fortune in the city. Hugh Meredith was friendly and liked to read; he also liked strong drink. Stephen Potts was a wit, willing but lazy. George Webb had come from England where he had attended Oxford. When he'd wearied of study, he went to London, spent his money, and then signed on as a bond servant to get to America. David Henry was hired as a "printer's devil" and had no ambition to better himself, while John, the errand boy, saved Ben trouble by running away.

Ben knew that he was fortunate to have three employees who really wished to learn their trade. Each day he taught them some new skill. He allowed them to stop work and watch while he cut new type to replace the broken pieces. Hugh got so interested that he stopped drinking. Stephen showed unsuspected abilities, and George took on tasks that relieved Ben.

There was another bit of good fortune that Ben didn't think of when he so quickly accepted his job. Keimer's had one advantage almost unheard of in the colonies—a five-day week. Because of his religious beliefs, Keimer allowed no work on Saturday. The law of Pennsylvania prohibited work on Sunday. So Ben had two days each week for reading and study. Soon the four men began having supper together two or three times a week. Often they lingered on, talking about books and pamphlets they had read.

"This is pleasant," Ben remarked one evening. "Let's start a club."

"A club?" George was astonished. "Could we?"

"Why not? We'd choose tradesmen, like ourselves—twelve, maybe."

"Did you ever hear of such a club?" Hugh asked.

"Well, not exactly." Ben hardly knew how the idea had come. "Cotton Mather had church societies. They organized to help each other in time of trouble. Here, we'd educate our-

selves; try to improve in reading and speaking and thinking.
Like the idea?"

They did. So they invited a carpenter, a glazier, a shoemaker, and a surveyor, and met to choose three or four more.
They planned to meet every Friday evening in a member's
house. Some named the group The Leather Apron Club, because they were working men, but Ben called it the Junto, a
word for a club from a Latin root meaning to join.

At the first meeting each man stood, alone, and put his
right hand on his breast as he promised to love mankind and
the truth; to help fellow-members and the colony; to study
subjects announced at meetings; and to write four papers each
year. Ben had a list of subjects ready—books, temperance, medi-
cal aid in illness, reasons for success or failure, how to become
a better man; they would not lack for topics.

Soon word got around; Philadelphia buzzed with talk
about the Junto, and others wanted to join. Two called at the
print shop.

"My neighbor and I would like to improve ourselves, Mr.
Franklin. We can read, but have no schooling. Will you
take us?"

"It is good to want to learn," Ben assured them. "But if
we take more than twelve, where shall we meet? How shall
every member have a chance to speak if there are twenty to hear
from?" When he saw the men's disappointment, a new idea
flashed into Ben's mind.

"Why don't you start a second club, Hugh?" he asked.
"Meet any evening but Friday. Would you men join with Hugh

Meredith?" They did, and the responsibility was good for Hugh. Soon George had a junto, too, and others were formed. Some were a passing fad, but several continued for years.

Late one afternoon of this same season, Keimer stumped up the stairs in a temper. "Is Mr. Logan's book ready?" he demanded.

"Yes, sir. I finished it myself ten minutes ago," Ben said. Tenderly he picked up a pamphlet he had bound in soft leather. The title was worked in gold; the tooling was perfect.

"If it is done, why have you not sent it?" Keimer shouted.

"Because I have no boy to send," Ben answered agreeably.

"No boy to send!" Keimer's face flushed hotly. "The richest man in the colony! The man with the best library in America tries out my shop to bind a book, and you 'have no boy'! Go yourself!"

"Yes, sir!" Ben whisked off his apron, wiped his hands. He wrapped the book carefully, and dashed off to Mr. Logan's house on Second Street before Keimer could change his mind.

Ben had never met Mr. Logan, but, like most Philadelphians, he knew the distinguished Quaker by sight. James Logan had come to Philadelphia in 1699 as secretary to William Penn. He was devoted to the Penn family and their interests. They paid him no salary, but he was allowed to trade in furs and land, and, being skillful, he had made quite a fortune. Part of his land was a large acreage five miles out on the Germantown road which he had named Stenton, after his father's home in Scotland. Ben had heard that Mr. Logan planned to build a house and live at Stenton some day. Fortunately, he was still in town and came to the door himself when Ben knocked.

"Oh, the new binding," he said. "Let me see the work."

Ben stepped inside—and then, as Logan took the parcel, he stared in amazement across the hall. Through an open door he saw a large, handsome room; shelves filled with books extended to the ceiling. Not even the biggest store in London had so many books!

"This is excellent workmanship," Logan was saying. "Who did it?"

"I did, sir. I'm Ben Franklin. I'm glad you like it."

"Like it!" Logan's voice was warm. "I didn't know anyone in Philadelphia could do so able a job. I'll send back three more for binding to match . . ." Then he glanced up and saw Ben's face.

"Oh, my library," he said, with quick understanding. "You love books." It was not a question. Ben's eyes had told him.

"Yes, sir. I've loved books ever since I can remember."

"I'm glad. And you are welcome to read mine. They will last you quite a while." His smile seemed to welcome Ben into that beautiful room. Ben paused on the threshold as Logan found the pamphlets to be bound. Candles burned; outside the sky was dark.

"A storm comes. Put these inside your shirt, Ben. You may take time to read these while you have them. And when you return them, bound, plan to stay an hour and tell me what you want to read."

"Thank you, sir. I'll have a care for these pamphlets." Ben tucked them away, and after a polite good-by, ran most of the way home to beat the storm.

That day's meeting opened a whole new world for Ben. Mr. Logan loaned him all the books he could read, evenings, and during his two precious days. Moreover the books were well selected, and Mr. Logan was willing to answer questions. Ben's inner life of studying and thinking, begun on the homeward voyage with Mr. Denham, grew steadily.

Then, too, leadership of the Junto challenged Ben to think and to write out his thoughts instead of dreaming. It was not easy to set down on paper ideas about God. How silly we were, back in Boston, Ben thought, to believe that we did not need God. Now he kept at the task until he got onto paper some of his beliefs.

There is one God, the Creator of all things.
God governs the world by His Providence.
God ought to be worshiped.
Doing good to man is the service most acceptable to God.

These thoughts clear in his mind, Ben next worked on prayers and worship ideas. These were very different from the litanies and sermons he had heard in Boston as a boy. Perhaps only in free-thinking Philadelphia could he have written as he did, for here, Quakers, Presbyterians, Baptists—and all others—worshiped as they believed.

As his pile of writing grew, Ben thought of the quality of his daily conduct—could he not make himself a better man? Each time he glimpsed Deborah on the street he remembered guiltily that he had failed her. He called that failure the Latin word *erratum,* his mistake, and wished he could make it right.

He ventured to call at the Reads', and after a brief stiffness, Mrs. Read and Deborah were friendly, and Ben's sense of guilt lightened. Encouraged, he thought on this. I try to make myself a better printer. Perhaps if I worked on my faults, I could make myself a better man.

Pulling a fresh sheet of paper toward him, he listed qualities he thought he should improve. To his distress he wrote down thirteen—without even stopping to think! Among the number were *frugality, silence, justice, humility, order, industry* . . . the column at the left of his paper lengthened, dismayingly. How could he work on so many faults at once?

Thirteen. I could work on a different one each week, he decided. He ruled the paper, took each quality in the order he had chanced to set it down, and scored himself on that each night—for seven days. Then he moved on to the next. At the end of a year, he thought perhaps he had made some progress toward the kind of man he wished to be. But the matter surely took faithful work!

Such quiet, orderly days, filled with work and study, were rudely interupted one winter morning. A noise in the street drew Ben to a window, and Keimer, coming up the stairs, saw him looking out.

"Do I pay you high wages to stare from my window?" Keimer shouted so loudly that people in the street heard. "I wish I had no contract! I would fire you at once!"

"Your wish is granted!" Franklin, flushed with embarrassment and temper, tore off his apron, dashed by Keimer and down the stairs.

"Hugh! Bring my things tonight!" he called over his shoulder.

A hushed silence held the printers. Who, now, would manage the shop, make ink and new type, manage customers, bind Mr. Logan's books?

That evening Hugh Meredith brought Ben's things and with them, a wonderful new idea.

"My father is in the city, Ben," he said. "He is pleased that I am learning a trade and have stopped drinking. He wants to set you and me up as partners in a print shop of our own. My share would be his money and my work; your share, skill and friends."

Ben could hardly believe the words he heard.

"You have a contract with Keimer till spring," he said.

"That's not long. And Keimer will be after you. Meanwhile, you like to read. Now you have a chance." Soon definite arrangements were made for the partnership, and Ben, glad he had saved enough to live on for a time, went to see Mr. Logan.

"I have a new book from London," Mr. Logan greeted him. "You like Defoe; this is his newest work—*The Complete English Tradesman*. Just your sort of book. Listen!" He led the way into the library, picked up the book, and read at random:

> "Trade is like a handmill; it must be turned by a diligent hand.
> "The shop says, 'keep me and I will keep thee.'
> "Nothing can give greater prospect of thriving, to a young tradesman, than his own diligence."

Logan glanced toward Ben. "Good, isn't it? I thought of you at once. In the back," he said, flipping pages, "is a section on how to keep books, to buy and sell."

"And I with no job, sir." Ben was chagrined, but he told Mr. Logan the story of his dismissal.

"Keimer'll be back for you. Meanwhile, be glad you have time to enjoy this new book."

Ben took it home and read it many times. It was a book he approved; he might have written it himself, had he the skill.

Keimer did come for Ben. He had a chance to print paper money for the colony of New Jersey. Ben was the only printer in either colony who knew how to engrave copper plate and to draw designs used to make imitation difficult. It was a task that challenged skill and soothed hurt vanity. Ben accepted. New Jersey law required that an official be present when money was printed, so Ben met many prominent men. They admired his skill and liked him. Weeks passed pleasantly.

Ben was twenty-two when, in the spring of 1728, he and Hugh opened their print shop on Water Street, near the river. The house was large, so they rented half to a Junto member and his wife, who agreed to board the partners for part of the rent. A Junto member brought them the first customer, a farmer who wanted a bit of printing done. The five shillings he paid seemed a small fortune—and the farmer was pleased, too.

Another Junto member wangled for them the job of printing a history of Quakers in America. Franklin promised to print at least one a day of the forty sheets planned. As their business grew, he often had to work at night to keep his promise.

"That Franklin works hard," men said, seeing his light.

Ben did not expect that a print shop would make him rich, not even in Philadelphia. But he hoped to earn a living in it. His first blow came from a friend and Junto member, George Webb.

"I thought you might have a job for me," Webb called to say.

"We haven't enough work for three—not yet," Ben replied.

"Later, maybe," George coaxed, standing by the press.

"Well," Ben hesitated, "Hugh and I talk of starting a newspaper. You know I wrote for one in Boston? We plan a lively one—entertaining."

"Bradford already has a paper," George said. "The *Mercury*."

"That dull thing! Ours would be different. Come around again, George. It might be—just maybe . . ."

George left. He went straight to Keimer and told him Ben's plans.

"Starts a paper, does he?" Keimer snorted. "Well, I'll start one first. You're hired, Webb."

Two months later he published *The Universal Instructor in Arts and Sciences and the Pennsylvania Gazette.*

"There's a name for you," Ben said. He had heard the sheet was coming. He bought and read a copy. Like Bradford's *Mercury,* it was dull—warmed-over London news, a speech by an assembly member, and advertisements. Ben went to see Bradford.

"I'd like to write a column of sprightly local news for the *Mercury,* Mr. Bradford," Ben offered. Bradford didn't know just what Ben meant, but he was frightened by new competition. Ben was hired. He called his column of friendly gossip, *The Busybody.* At first he tried to disguise—more or less—those he wrote about. But he soon learned that people *liked* to read about themselves in the paper, and, as in the "Silence Dogood" papers, he was skillful in stopping before the end of a tale. "More next time . . ." he would write.

Keimer had no gift for writing and could not find a rival to Ben. His paper began to fail; his debts to mount. In the autumn of 1729, he sold his shop to an apprentice, his paper to Franklin, and left for the West Indies.

"What will you do now?" Hugh exclaimed. The partners had not expected events to happen so rapidly.

"I'll drop that outlandish name," Franklin planned. "I'll call the sheet *The Pennsylvania Gazette* and go right on publishing. Bradford will have to find a new writer, and we'll have the best paper in the colonies."

The Library Company

The Pennsylvania Gazette pleased its readers. It was newsy and easy to read, being cleanly printed with good type. Ben developed a knack at cutting small pictures to draw attention to an article or an advertisement.

"Never heard of a picture in a newspaper!" a reader said.

"I'll wager no other newspaper in the colonies has pictures," another boasted. "That Franklin is a man for venturing."

The editor's lively columns, without malice, intrigued readers in local affairs. Papers were watched for and passed from person to person. But there were few subscribers.

Bradford's *Mercury* was duller than ever without Franklin's feature—but the paper was delivered promptly. He was the postmaster, and so had carriers; that attracted paid advertising. Ben, with only ninety subscribers, had to hire men to deliver in evenings or at odd times.

Since the *Gazette* was growing slowly, Ben was eager to

*Sloth makes all
things difficult,
but industry all easy.*

get more printing business; he wanted a contract to print paper money for Pennsylvania. The colony needed paper money; his work had pleased in New Jersey—why not in his own colony?

There was difference of opinion as to whether paper money was a good thing. Wealthy men had hard money—coins of gold and silver. Common people had no money; they must barter when they bought and sold—a hog for an iron pot, feathers for pins. Many thought a reasonable amount of paper money would be good for all.

The Junto debated the question at several meetings. Franklin wrote a paper he called "A Modest Inquiry into the Nature and Necessity of Paper Currency." He read it at a meeting, listened carefully to comments, and rewrote parts he thought he could improve. Then he printed the paper and distributed it.

As men read it many thought his points were reasonable— "A colony needs money to carry on trade; Pennsylvania has less than needed." His arguments were ingenious, and he begged every reader to think of the good of the whole colony.

The topic of paper money came to be debated in taverns and on the streets. Franklin's effort to make economic principles clear to all made a deep impression. Then he had another idea.

When the governor made his annual address to the Pennsylvania Assembly, Franklin got it and printed the whole speech. He used excellent paper; the type was elegant and the printing neat. He gave a free copy to each of the assembly members.

"This was printed by Benjamin Franklin, the man who wrote about paper money," his friends reminded assemblymen.

Franklin's ideas and his printing, aided by the prodding of merchants and farmers who longed for paper money, induced the assembly to pass a bill ordering a limited amount of paper currency—printed by Benjamin Franklin.

Through that winter of 1729-30, while Ben worked faithfully on the printing business and the *Gazette,* he thought constantly of Deborah. He did not lack for chances to meet attractive young women, but none seemed Deborah's equal in looks and manner.

So on the first day of September, 1730, they were married. The tenant in half the big house on Water Street had moved away; Ben and his wife began housekeeping there. "Debbie," Ben's name for his wife, was now gay and happy; she was also a good cook and housewife.

Like other women of the time, she had no formal education, but she was intelligent and quick to learn. She picked up some reading and writing. She learned how to stitch paper together to make a pamphlet. When Ben opened a stationery store in a front room downstairs, she kept shop. Her friendly manner and pretty face helped make it successful. At first the shop carried paper, parchment, ink, lampblack, and a few small books. As trade grew Franklin added soap, goosefeathers, and other things he got in trade.

The next year son William played in a cradle in the shop, amusing customers by his bright ways. A woman who kept shop and tended home and baby was unusual in Philadelphia; Deborah enjoyed her double role.

As for Ben, he bought rags, delivered them in his wheelbarrow, bringing back supplies of paper—with no loss of dignity. The new Christ Church opened, and the Franklins had a pew, in the middle, left of the aisle. They were respected members of the community.

Through busy months when work and home absorbed him, Ben managed to continue reading books borrowed from Mr. Logan. The beautiful house at Stenton, begun in 1727, was

finally finished, and the Logans had moved out from the town
the year Ben was married. Not long after Ben met him, Mr.
Logan had been sadly crippled by a fall on the ice; he had to
give up many activities and so could spend hours with Ben in
the handsome second-floor library, talking about ideas and
books. The knowledge Ben got and the inspiration of Mr. Logan's company were well worth the five-mile walk to Stenton.
Ben went as often as possible.

Then, too, he kept his pledge to read, debate, and write
for the Junto. Other juntos that organized called themselves
The Union, The Band, and various names, and did well enough.
But none was more faithful than that first Junto, The Leather
Apron Club. Its problem was to get books on subjects members
wished to study—philosophy, natural science, economics, history.

Most of the members had one or two or three books. They
decided to keep these at the home of Robert Grace, where they
met each Friday evening.

"We might allow a member to take a book home to read,"
Franklin suggested. "He could return it at the next meeting."
So it was agreed. He wished that they might all read books
he borrowed from Mr. Logan. But when, after some months,
members found that their books were worn and two were lost,
Ben was glad he had not suggested more borrowing.

But the Junto still needed books.

Ben remembered that library of secondhand books in London. By paying a small fee he was allowed to take a book home
and read it carefully. This was much better than the over-night

borrowing he had done in Boston, where he must read all night to finish. In London he took his time.

Perhaps, Ben thought, if several of us club together, we can buy books and loan them to each other. A small yearly fee would replace lost or damaged books and pay for new ones. He got out pencil and paper and began to figure.

"If a hundred men each paid two pounds sterling, that sum would buy many books," he said aloud as he wrote. "Then if each paid ten shillings a year—you know, Debbie, I think I have a good idea."

Debbie smiled and agreed; of course the idea was good. It was Ben's.

But when Ben presented the plan to friends, very few wanted to pay two pounds sterling just for *books*. Philadelphians did not care *that* much for reading.

A few evenings later Ben had a new thought.

"I think I've told this too much as my own idea," he said to Deborah. "I should put myself in the background. Tomorrow, as I meet a man I wish to interest, I shall say, 'Friends of mine are working on a library project and would like you to help make it a success.'"

This venture in diplomacy was so successful that soon Ben had fifty subscribers—not the hundred he wanted, but enough for a start. The next time he went to Stenton he appealed to Mr. Logan for advice in selecting books to be bought.

"I'll be glad to help," Logan said. "Bring a list of subjects you wish to study, and I'll suggest books. You'll have to order from London—do you know anyone there?"

"I thought maybe Mr. Peter Collinson might be willing to buy for us, sir. I met him in London."

"You couldn't do better," Mr. Logan approved. "He is my friend, too. He will take a deep interest, I know."

In July of 1731, a legal plan for The Library Company of Philadelphia was drawn up and signed. Money was paid in, and directors appointed. But as all were busy men, the first order for books was not actually sent until the next March.

This done at last and his own business going well, it was a shock to Ben to learn that Mr. Meredith's affairs had changed and that he could not pay the last hundred pounds due on the purchase of the press and type. Moreover, Hugh brooded over his father's failure and was drinking again. This double blow came just when Ben was encouraged by a few new subscribers and advertisers.

"I can't give up now!" he exclaimed to Hugh. 'I *won't!*"

"My father really cannot pay," Hugh said sadly. "I hated to tell you, Ben. I'm leaving Philadelphia. I am a weight on you here. I was brought up on a farm; I'll be better off in the country . . ."

"But, Hugh! I need you here!"

"Thank you, Ben, for those words. But I am going. Some Welsh friends are settling in North Carolina—perhaps I'll amount to something there."

Ben saw that his friend and partner had made his decision; he could but agree. He tried to put his distress aside as he wished Hugh good fortune. His own future looked dark, indeed.

On an evening after Hugh left, two friends came to call.

"We came separately to see you, Ben," one said. "We met at your door. Now we find our business is the same."

"Come in, come in," Ben invited, though puzzled at their words.

"We hear that you are having business troubles," the other man said. "We have been prospering; we offer you a loan for as much as you may need to set things right."

Franklin could not speak. The generous offer, so unexpected, meant even more to him than money—important as that was. These friends offered him faith—in himself and in his paper.

"How can I thank you?" he cried, his face flushed with joy.

"We ask no thanks, Ben. Your paper is good for Philadelphia. We are friends. Now tell us how much you need."

Ben figured—the hundred pounds now due, a few small debts, some supplies he must have—"Two hundred pounds?"

"Write the notes, and the money is yours." Ben signed, agreeing to pay the debt as business grew.

"We'll not hurry you," they said generously.

"You will see, my friends," Ben said, as they left, "I will show my appreciation by making my paper the best in the colony."

Now that he no longer worried, he worked with a free mind, and new ideas flowed. But he was cautious, too. Because he suspected subscribers might think him young to run a paper alone, he bided his time for announcing the change in partnership. The first issue of the *Gazette* with "B. Franklin" as sole publisher was dated May 11, 1732.

Now, with the paper successful, Ben could pay the money due to Mr. Vernon. Brother John's friend had been patient; only once had he written about the debt, and then Ben had replied honestly that he had spent some and could not repay the debt just then. It was a wonderful relief to be free of that haunting worry.

Never again, Ben vowed, will I touch money not my own!

A few mornings later, as he sat down to eat breakfast, his usual meal of porridge and milk was in a new china bowl. By it was a shining silver spoon, the first silver spoon Ben had ever had in his house.

"Where is my pottery bowl, Debbie? Where is the pewter spoon?"

"Here. At my place—see?" Deborah laughed at his surprise. "I decided that the time had come for my husband to eat with silver from china—and I have so arranged it." Franklin laughed, enjoying his breakfast the more because of her pride in him.

The Franklins' second son was born in October of that busy year, and Ben named him Francis Folger Franklin for his mother's father, a well-educated and successful man of Nantucket. Deborah was pleased. In a few days she was keeping shop again, watching run-around Will and showing off handsome little Franky to interested customers. Ben, in his happiness, worked harder than ever.

As though all that was not enough excitement, the boxes of library books arrived in a few days. Such an evening as that was when the volumes were unpacked and set on the shelves prepared in Lewis Timothy's house in Pewter Platter Alley!

Franklin unpacked his favorite Defoe and his gifts to the library, a print of the Magna Charta and Montaigne's *Essays*. As a surprise, Peter Collinson had included Sir Isaac Newton's book, *Principles,* and a book on gardening.

"I didn't realize we would have so many," Franklin said, as they stood back and admired their collection. "I'll print a list so that we can each have it at home."

"We'll need to open the rooms twice a week—how about Wednesday and Saturday, Lewis?"

The library delighted its subscribers. The next year more books were bought; so the library was moved to Robert Grace's home, and Ben was elected librarian. He printed new lists and gave so many hours of work to the library that members voted he should pay no dues for two years. Recognition of his work gave Ben more pleasure than the money saved.

As news of the Library Company got around, many called the project the first library in America. They forgot, or perhaps they did not know, that Harvard, Yale, William and Mary, and perhaps other colleges had libraries. But these were different. Colleges were to train ministers; so their libraries were about theology. The Library Company was the first to be organized by artisans and mechanics for their own improvement. Only those who subscribed were allowed to take books home, but during the hours the room was open anyone might come in and read. In this sense it was the first "public" library. From the start, it was a success.

"If we are not careful, we'll make reading fashionable,"

Ben remarked to Deborah. *She* knew that the idea was his— and most of the work. Outside, he was careful to give credit to the subscribers.

Though Philadelphia did not have the reputation of being literary, like Boston, it was the most important city in the colonies. Good climate and location on a wide river made it a fine place for commerce. From its wharves, goods went by pack-horse to wilderness settlers. But the character of the founder, William Penn, was the most important factor in its growth.

Quaker Penn was a just man with liberal views on worship. His fairness to Indians resulted in safety to farm settlers. His wisdom made the colony and city thrive and prosper; it became a center of immigration from Europe.

In the early 1730's, when Benjamin Franklin began to prosper, the city extended about a mile along the river and a half mile back toward the forest. The wide main street that Penn named High Street, as in any proper English village, had so many market stalls that people spoke of it as Market Street, and forgot its early name.

Christ Church was one of the very beautiful churches in the new world. Houses were red brick, gay against the forest green. Each had its garden, its doorstone and flagstone walk. Shops were in a front room of a merchant's house, and his sign, an anchor, a beehive, a bell, hung by the front door. Orchards thrived. A visitor from England wrote, "Ripe peaches are fed to the hogs, while at home they are worth their weight in gold!"

Pennsylvania had no specialty for shipping, such as tobacco, rice, codfish. She shipped what she had—wheat, beef, pork, butter, apples, cheese, candles, soap, starch, hair powder, drugs and herbs, shingles and barrel staves—all to be sold for hard money.

Shippers developed a triangle of trade—to the West Indies or to Spain or Portugal; then, with empty bottoms and chests of cash, ships sailed to England to load goods ordered months before and consigned to Philadelphia. Of course, there were variations; some ships went only to the West Indies and returned with molasses, cotton, sugar. Others went direct to England. But most took the triangle that fed West Indians, kept English artisans prosperous, and provided the colony with manufactured goods.

Philadelphians worked hard and prospered. Few were poor, fewer rich or aristocratic; that was why Ben, who wore his leather apron daily, was welcome at Mr. Logan's and other homes.

In this commercial city the trade of a printer would have seemed a poor way to make a living. But Franklin, by his ingenuity and diligence, made a living and a place for himself. And steadily, year by year, he educated himself and widened his acquaintance and his thinking. It was hard work; but he enjoyed each day.

Stenton

"Poor Richard"

The year 1732, when Benjamin Franklin was twenty-six, was an important time for the young printer. His *Pennsylvania Gazette* was growing. The Library Club flourished, little Franky was healthy and bright, and, as the year moved toward its end, Ben launched a new project—the printing of an almanac.

Several almanacs were published in the colonies. The little booklets were calendars for the coming year and, in addition, listed movements of the stars, sun and moon, the tides, and other bits of information. Franklin knew that he took a risk in publishing a new booklet late in the fall—people would have bought Bradford's or some other. And once an almanac was hanging on the kitchen chimney, who would wastefully buy a second one? But he chanced December printing.

Franklin's almanac was small, slightly more than three by six inches. Its cover was pale green with gay pink and red flowers. Inside, as a preface, was a letter signed by a fictitious "Richard

Early to bed, early to rise,
makes a man healthy,
wealthy, and wise.

Saunders" who frankly announced his true motive in publishing an almanac:

"The plain truth of the matter is that I am excessively poor and my wife, good woman, is, I tell her, excessively proud. She cannot bear to sit spinning in her shift of tow while I gaze at the stars." The printer, Saunders confided, had offered him a share in the profits. So—here was the almanac.

The pages following the preface had the usual calendar of each month with the hour of sunrise and sunset; the movements of moon and tides and planets. Near the back was a list of historic dates—the birth of Jesus, the Roman capture of Jerusalem, the building of the Tower of London—and a list of English kings. The printing was neat, the stitching perfect.

On a December afternoon boys ran along the street peddling the almanac—price, five pence. A few men bought out of curiosity. Here and there a purchaser began to read—and to chuckle.

"Good, is it? Here, boy! I'll take one!"

Soon several men loitered along, reading. Franklin's easy style was well known through the *Gazette;* there was no Richard Saunders in town. Word passed along—"Ben wrote this!"

"Poor Richard!" one reader mocked, laughing. "Now if he only had a good industrious wife like Mrs. Franklin . . ."

By evening the first modest edition was sold; Franklin worked most of the night printing more copies. Before the new year began, he had printed and sold three editions—and was as amazed as anyone at his own success.

As he reprinted, ideas for the next year flowed through his

mind. I'll have Richard thank the good people for getting his
wife new shoes and a dress, he planned. He'll assure them that
now he has a secondhand coat, he may walk on the street.

The name, "Poor Richard," given laughingly, stuck through
years. That almanac became the best known of any in the colonies. The immediate effect of its success was to give Ben Franklin something he had never before enjoyed—spare cash. And he
knew exactly what he wanted to do with it.

Because of the flow of commerce in and out of Philadelphia,
Franklin was in touch with several cities in the colonies. The
Gazette was well known, and he had been asked to publish such
a paper—Charleston, South Carolina, especially, wanted a good
newspaper. Now he had capital to supply that need.

The question was whom should he send to print and publish, and what business arrangements should he make? The
name of Lewis Timothy came to mind—the man who helped
with the Library Company books.

Lewis was a well-trained journeyman printer in whom
Franklin had confidence. As Louis Timothée, a French Protes-
tant, he had fled to Holland and there married a Hollander.
When they came to Philadelphia, he used the English form of
his name, easier for his new friends. Franklin met him when
he came to the *Gazette* to advertise for pupils to study French.

Franklin had taught himself German and was doing some
job printing for German colonists; he had tried out a German
newspaper (the first in America), but found delivery problems
too difficult at the time. Now he promptly took this chance to
study French. He had no plan for using this language, nor Span-

ish, nor Italian, nor Latin, which he learned after he mastered French—he simply had a craving to learn. Study was pleasure; printing was his business.

Franklin talked with Timothy about a Charleston *Gazette,* and the Frenchman was excited by the prospect.

"We won't form a partnership," Franklin explained. "I think it is better that you have full charge from the first. I'll agree to set you up and pay one third of the cost each year; you pay me one third of the profits. After six years, you have the right to buy the press and type at a fair price."

"That's very generous, Mr. Franklin," Timothy said, gratefully. They wrote out this agreement, and both signed. Soon the Timothys left for Charleston. The paper he established was so successful that soon other papers, the *Connecticut Gazette* and the *New York Gazette* among them, were started with the same sound business arrangement. In the years since the failure of his friendship for John Collins and James Ralph, Franklin had pondered on how to form good friendships and choose employees. He felt that his study now rewarded him. The men he chose for newspaper work proved their worth.

Even as these newspaper arrangements were going on, Franklin proceeded with his second project financed by almanac cash; a visit to his family in Boston. Ben had kept in touch with his kinfolk; many colonials never saw or heard from families after leaving home. Ben had written letters and got replies. He sold Crown Soap that John and Peter made in Newport, and they sold books he printed. Brother James, Ben's one-time employer, had moved his print shop to Newport, where he did the official printing for Rhode Island and published an almanac. Ben wanted to see them all; but first, of course, his parents.

In August of 1733, Ben gave Deborah power of attorney so she could manage his business. Then he left for Boston. The young man of twenty-seven who now journeyed north was quite different from the confident youth who, nine years earlier, had come with Governor Keith's letter. Now Ben was married and had two sons. His business prospered. He had a wide and growing acquaintance in the colonies. And he was truly modest, ripened by experience.

The house at Union and Hanover seemed little changed, but the people looked older than Ben had expected. And in the city, he missed the easy ways of Philadelphia.

Jane Franklin Mecom lived in Boston, so he went to see her.

"Oh, Ben!" Her eyes shone as she drew him into the house. "See the spinning wheel you sent me? It has seen good service making clothing for my family—as you knew it would. And here is Ben, your namesake!"

Franklin laid his arm across the shoulders of a sturdy lad. "Mother says that when I am old enough, you may let me come to Philadelphia and learn printing from you, Uncle Ben."

"You shall be my apprentice, then my partner," his uncle promised. They had a wonderful day together.

Returning, Ben stopped for several days in Newport. He visited with John and Peter and their families and made peace with James. It was a shock to find this brother ill. The printing business was run by his wife and two daughters, who were twelve and fourteen years old. His son was younger.

"You are the first women printers I have heard of," Ben said with frank admiration.

"Necessity is a good teacher," Mrs. James Franklin said.

"But women working . . ." Suddenly Ben thought of the work that Deborah did; of his trust while he was on this journey. He told his relatives of her skillful ways. "Franklins marry good wives," he said. On the last evening, James had a serious talk with Ben.

"As you can see, Brother, I am not long for this world. I wish that my son, Jemmy, had been born earlier so that I could teach him . . ." He paused for breath and Ben waited, heartsick to see him suffer. "When I am gone, will you take care of him, Ben? Will you teach him?"

"That I shall!" Ben promised. "Send him to me now—or any time you think right. He's ten, didn't you say? I'll give him schooling and teach him our trade. He can come back here and run your shop. That's what you want, isn't it, James?"

The boy's face glowed. He could not imagine his father gone, so the idea of going to Philadelphia was thrilling.

As he left for home, Ben Franklin had a happy feeling about his family. This trip had been worth making. As for those he had visited, they talked often of him.

"Who would have thought that Ben would turn out so well," John marveled. "He has made the printing business get him clothes and travel—I never heard of a printer doing that well."

"But we must remember, brothers," Peter said, "that Ben

was different, even as a lad. Did we read books nights? Did we eat little to save money—not to keep in a sock but to buy books? It is not chance that makes him now a well known man. He has worked. And all the while grown more modest."

"That is true," John agreed. "It is strange—and good, both."

"I'm glad he came," James admitted. "I feel at peace."

The returned traveler was refreshed by his journey and worked with new zeal. He printed more books; religious works, because most men who bought books were interested in theology.

Fellow citizens showed their confidence in him by electing him to public offices, clerk of the assembly and postmaster of Philadelphia. Neither of these offices carried much distinction, but Franklin was pleased to be chosen; the clerkship brought the right to print official papers for the colony, and the post-mastership provided carriers for the *Gazette*.

The household near the market was a busy and happy one those early years of the 1730's. Improved prosperity brought modest comforts, but Franklin's joy was in his family. His sons were bright, healthy lads. William had started to school, and Franky toddled around the store and shop, smiling, and curious about everything he saw.

Then came the hardest blow of Benjamin Franklin's life.

The summer of 1736 was hot, and a terrible epidemic of smallpox spread over the city. Everyone who could left town. Those who must stay risked inoculation rather than the loath-some sickness.

When Ben Franklin was writing for the *New England*

Courant, he made fun of the "newfangled notion," inoculation. Actually, he knew nothing about medicine and did not bother to inform himself. Cotton Mather and others were for it, so Ben was against it. With fifteen years of living and learning, Ben had changed. Now the *Gazette* advised inoculation. It informed readers of the low death rate—only six of two hundred who had been inoculated had died.

But Ben could not bring himself to inoculate little Franky: the serum was not perfected. Some who took it died. Of course he meant to inoculate the lad—tomorrow.

Franky caught smallpox. He died, horribly—only four years old. Franklin felt that he never, oh, never, could forgive himself for neglect. The grieving father had carved on the small tombstone the words, "The delight of all who knew him."

As autumn came, the epidemic passed, and the stricken city stirred toward recovery. In work Franklin found comfort. And he again spent twelve hours each week in reading, study, and observation of nature.

Not long after Franky's death, Brother James died, and young James came to live with the Franklins. Uncle Ben kept his promise; he sent him to school, treated him like a son, and taught him printing.

In the late 1730's, George Whitefield, an evangelist, came to Philadelphia. His brilliant oratory drew large audiences; Franklin was fascinated by his preaching. But he did not always agree with his ideas for using large collections given by audiences for the good preacher's charities. Because Ben disagreed, he sometimes refused to contribute.

"I happened to attend one of his sermons," he wrote later, "in the course of which I perceived he intended to finish with a collection, and I silently resolved he should get nothing from me. I had in my pocket a handful of copper money, three or four silver dollars, and five pistoles in gold. As he proceeded, I began to soften, and concluded to give the coppers. Another stroke of his oratory made me ashamed of that, and determined me to give the silver; and he finished so admirably that I emptied my pocket wholly into the collector's dish, gold and all."

A poor speaker himself, Ben found Whitefield's flow of words, the rich tones of his voice, a miracle. He heard that Whitefield preached to thousands at a time, one day to 25,000. Franklin wondered, was that possible? He decided to find out. While the preacher was speaking to a large crowd in Market Street, Ben backed away until street noises made him lose the sound of Whitefield's voice. Then he stepped off the distance to the speaker. He took that distance for a radius and figured the space in half a circle. Allowing two square feet standing room for a person, he figured on a bit of paper. Why, the report was correct! Right there in Market Street, 30,000 people could hear that wonderful voice!

This proof of Whitefield's powerful voice so fascinated Franklin that when it was proposed the city erect a building for the evangelist, so that services could go on in bad weather, he was eager to help. He made but one condition; the building must be free for a speaker of *any* faith. If a Turk came and wished to explain Mohammedanism, he was to be welcomed and allowed to speak there. The challenge was accepted, and the new church became the first undenominational church in America.

Meanwhile the *Gazette* and *Poor Richard* continued to thrive. Remembering how much he liked the axioms in Defoe's *English Tradesman,* Franklin wrote short axioms for the almanac. He kept them on slips of paper in a box, and when, in making up the pages of the almanac, he found a little space, he selected an axiom to fit it.

> "Search others for their virtues, thyself for thy vices."
> "To the boiling pot, flies come not."
> "A penny saved is a penny got."
> "Spare and have is better than spend and crave."
> "A good example is the best sermon."
> "There is no little enemy."
> "He that cannot obey cannot command."

There was no pretense that the ideas were original; some were the wisdom of generations. Some were remembered bits from Defoe or perhaps from Swift, or other authors Ben had read. But all were expressed in Ben's terse, pithy phrases—original in that sense.

Gradually he made changes in the format of the almanac, too. He inserted blank pages between the months so that the owner could write down his own events: births, deaths, travels, and family happenings. He published a pocket almanac an inch and three quarters by four and a quarter—the size to slip into a coat pocket. This had a monthly calendar and little else, but was handy to carry and so was popular.

As he prospered, Franklin began to think of what service

he could do for his city. The streets were filthy—a disgrace to homes where steps and doorsills were scrubbed daily. Franklin hunted up a man who was willing to sweep Market Street (as a beginning) twice a week and carry off the trash in a cart. So he went from house to house with his idea.

"Will you pay a few pennies a month to have your street clean?" he'd ask politely.

"Of course we will, Mr. Franklin! Why didn't someone think of this long ago?" Gradually the plan was accepted, and other streets were cleaned.

Next he improved the night watch by hiring only honest men as watchmen. Perhaps the most quickly successful venture was the organization of a fire department.

Franklin remembered from his youth the shocking losses from great fires. Boston was having some success with volunteer firemen—why not Philadelphia? He began his campaign by short articles in the *Gazette*.

"Cover embers on the shovel when you carry coals to light a fire in another room," he advised. And "keep wooden trim away from the front of the fireplace."

He wrote a paper for the Junto on organizing a fire department, and after he read it to them, he listened carefully to improvements suggested.

Then he organized the Union Fire Company, which was an immediate success. Each member promised to keep six or more leather buckets on hand and to have handy sacks in which possessions could safely and quickly be carried from a burning house. Members met socially once a month and discussed ways of fighting fire.

In this way, printer Franklin added civic work to his busy days. Ere long he became known as a public-spirited citizen as well as a tradesman and printer.

Franklin's Kite

One of the important traits of Benjamin Franklin's personality was his curiosity. Every day he observed new wonders; every day he longed for more time to observe and to think. There should be quicker ways to do chores so that more time could be used for reading and study. Labor saving was not a topic of interest in the colonies; labor was cheap. New workers came on every ship.

Walking by the fireplace one day, Franklin noticed the little maid whose duty it was to stand by the hot fire and turn the spit as the meat browned. How wasteful to use a person, even a girl, when the wind was so powerful! After some thought he cut a small hole in the wall, set a little windmill in it, connected that with the spit, and presto—the wind did the turning!

Next time meat was roasting, the maid was doing pleasanter work—and somehow the air in the room had a fresh smell. Ben smiled as he went on to a Junto meeting.

The ancients tell us what is best; but we must learn from the moderns what is fittest.

This meeting was to arrange for observing an eclipse of the moon, due the next Friday evening at nine o'clock. But alas for their good planning—not a thing could be seen! A storm covered the sky two hours before the eclipse was due.

Later, when Boston papers came, Franklin read a long description of the eclipse.

"Could this be true?" He marveled to his helper. "Or is it imagined, written before the day? I shall ask my sister."

"The eclipse was over two hours before the storm broke," Jane wrote in reply. This set Ben to watching and jotting down the time and direction of storms—in Philadelphia, and as reported elsewhere by the newspapers. The facts he collected showed that most storms moved from the southwest to the northeast. His records were the first accurate observations of their kind.

As autumn neared, Mrs. Franklin, as usual, ordered wood. "It is costly stuff this year, Ben," she complained.

"Our town is growing," Ben reminded her. "When people move in, the forest moves back, making a long haul for the load."

"We should burn less, then," Deborah said thriftily. "But even with that big fireplace, we are often cold. Such drafts!"

This was enough to set Ben thinking. He studied that fireplace, noting the drafts, the amount of wood, the muss, ever needing to be brushed clean with a turkey wing. He drew a sketch; for several days he studied it, making improvements. Then he took the design to his Junto friend, Robert Grace, who earned his living with his iron furnace. Grace studied it.

"I never saw the like of this—will it work, Ben?"

"Make it, and we shall see. No blame to you if it doesn't.
Hot air will be reflected out; cold air comes down the chimney . . ."

"Yes, yes. It *sounds* good. 'Twill be a wood saver if it
works."

The stove was a success. Curious visitors were delighted
with the warm room, tidy hearth, the small amount of wood
needed. Grace made himself a stove—he called it "Franklin's

stove." The governor ordered one. Soon Grace had more orders than he could fill.

"I like your stove, Mr. Franklin," the governor said, when he met the inventor on the street. "I'll give you an order for a patent on it. You can make something on each stove."

"I thank your honor; I gave my sketches to Robert Grace. He earns his living in iron; I'm a printer. Every day I enjoy ideas of men who have lived before me—we all do. If I, in my turn, can think of something to help others, it is only fair that I give it without gain to myself."

The governor was astonished. This Franklin had unusual ideas.

Franklin appreciated his government offices. But the clerkship required tedious hours of sitting at a desk taking notes of assembly business.

One day when arguments were long, idleness oppressed Ben. He chanced to remember a game of numbers he had invented. At school he had failed in arithmetic, and after a time, he decided failure was silly. He made up the game to get numbers into his head. Why not try it now? He pulled a paper toward him.

On the blank page he drew a large square, then divided it into small squares—8 across, 8 down. Then, thinking hard, he began writing numbers in the 64 small squares. The confusion of the assembly room vanished in his pleasure in the game.

There, it figured out. Add any column up and down and it was 260; crosswise, 260. He drew a line from the lower left-

hand corner to the center, then to the lower righthand corner;
squares touched made 260. The time flew. When the debate
ended, and he must record the vote, he was refreshed—because he had used his mind. After that day he often played with
numbers in the squares or circles.

Someone chanced to see the squares and mentioned the matter to Mr. Logan, who requested Franklin to send him samples.
Next time Ben went to Stenton, Logan showed him a similar
game published by a French mathematician. Logan also wrote
to Peter Collinson about Ben's game:

> "Our Ben Franklin is certainly an extraordinary man, one
> of singular good judgment and modesty. He is clerk of our
> assembly and there, for want of other employment while he sat
> idle, he took it into his head to think of *magical squares,* in
> which he outdid Frenicle himself."

But to Ben the squares remained just an amusing game.

52	61	4	13	20	29	36	45
14	3	62	51	46	35	30	19
53	60	5	12	21	28	37	44
11	6	59	54	43	38	27	22
55	58	7	10	23	26	39	42
9	8	57	56	41	40	25	24
50	63	2	15	18	31	34	47
16	1	64	49	48	33	32	17

As Philadelphia grew, the mail grew, too. Often the "post-office"—a corner of the print shop—was piled high. Franklin read so many newspapers that he came to have a feeling of belonging to the whole new world, not just one colony.

"We ought to have a club for all the colonies," he remarked at a Junto meeting. "A few of us here, one or two each from New York, Boston, Charleston, Burlington—or any colonial town. We could compare our observations and new ideas."

"How could we meet, Ben?"

"We wouldn't have to meet. We could exchange letters."

"Well, then, write a few and try it out," the Junto agreed.

Ben wrote to a selected list of men; the response was slow, but in time the feeble beginning grew into the American Philosophical Society, with Franklin as its president.

About this same time, Franklin helped to organize a hospital to care for immigrants who became ill aboard ship or after arrival. It, too, was a new idea that lived on.

By 1743, when Franklin was thirty-seven, his mind, his days, and his household were so filled with projects and people that only a man of his genius could have enjoyed himself. His positions, his inventions, his observations and records, his *Gazette* and almanac, and his wide correspondence occupied his thoughts. In his home, apprentices, employees, relatives, and family kept Deborah busy through long days. James's son, Jemmy, was there, and Jane's Benny. Ben's only daughter, Sarah, a beautiful child, was born that year. David Hall of London accepted Ben's invitation to come and work in the shop—he relieved Ben, but added to the household.

To give himself a change, Franklin decided to visit Boston again. It had grown, too, he found. A fine new building, Faneuil Hall, was being finished at the foot of Union Street. It changed the look of the neighborhood. The old apothecary's shop was now a feather store, with feathers piled inside the windows instead of handsome bottles. Franklin visited with his family and listened to talk of war. Europe was a vast battlefield; France and Spain against England, Holland and Austria. Colonial port cities, he heard, feared invasion.

"Isn't Philadelphia preparing for attack?" he was asked.

"We have many Quakers," he said. "And we are too indifferent."

When business took him to Boston again three years later, he was astonished to see the vast defense preparations. And his own city had nothing! A single armed privateer might come up the river and take over Philadelphia!

As soon as he was at home, he wrote and published a stirring pamphlet entitled *Plain Truth,* pointing out dangers.

After there was time for the pamphlet to be read, Franklin called a public meeting, and, in one of his rare speeches, he urged action for defense. His arguments were so sound that 1200 men enlisted at once. Thousands signed up later. Cannon were ordered. With these installed on the river bank, even Quakers felt easier. Young William, with a few others, enlisted and served in New England.

Benjamin Franklin was recognized as the leader in this defense work. The governor, the assembly, the leading citizens and common folk turned to him. Their faith was deepened

by knowledge that he served the common good and asked nothing for himself.

During this time, study was not forgotten. Each year, when
Mr. Collinson sent the order of books for the Library Company,
he added a few as gifts. In the middle 1740's several of these
were on the subject of electricity—it was not a new topic, only
new in Philadelphia.

During the busy winter of 1746-7,' Franklin read about
electricity. It was a fascinating change from his scores of practical interests. Evenings, he often made simple experiments.
Word got around, and his room was ofttimes crowded with
men watching spellbound when he got a spark by rubbing a
piece of glass or a bit of amber. For years experimenters had
been doing these same things but had come to no conclusions.
Experiments were thought of as amusing tricks.

When the library books came in 1747, Mr. Collinson's gift
was not books. He sent a glass tube, thirty inches long, wide
enough to grasp.

"What is it?" an astonished member exclaimed.

"It's a Leyden jar," Ben cried. "Mr. Spence in Boston has
one! Look! Rub it . . ."

"Here's a book tells of it," another member noticed.

"Spence said that three men in Leyden, Holland, discovered
how to make such a tube. It stores up electricity made by rubbing—"

"The book says to rub the glass with cloth or buckskin
and hold the tube against the thing to be charged."

"Now we have something important to experiment with!"

Ben sighed happily. The print shop was packed evenings after that, as men dropped in to watch the strange magic of that glass tube.

To most of these, it was a fascinating toy. But four men, including Franklin, began serious study and experimenting.

As the year 1748 came in, and with it Franklin's forty-second birthday, he began to study his own life, much as he had twenty years earlier. His print shop surged with people, morning, noon, and night. Talk was on defense, the hospital, the Junto, news for the *Gazette*, the fire department, street cleaning, improvements he made in the stove, the postoffice, the assembly, the Pennsylvania Academy—there seemed no end to the number and range of his affairs. Everything interested him—but did he want to use his whole life this way? What *did* he want? What did he want *most?*

I want a simpler life, he told himself. I want time to read and to swim, time to linger at my meal, to think. I have no desire for wealth—surely I have enough money to live simply. I shall retire—and enjoy my life.

The decision made, he acted. He sold the *Gazette* to David Hall for one thousand pounds a year for eighteen years. He bought a house and land at the corner of Second Street and Sassafras—far enough out to deter casual visitors. His land extended to the river. He could sit on the bank with a book or a friend, or swim an hour, or observe nature—a study of ants was to be one of his first projects. Deborah and the children liked the house and its setting. William, home from war service, was a popular beau; Sally, a pretty, agreeable little girl. The nephews were away, Jemmy with his paper in Newport, Benny in the West Indies. Franklin felt a serene happiness—*now* he could study.

Even before he made these changes, Franklin had written to Mr. Collinson about electricity:

"I never before engaged in any study that so totally engrossed my attention and my time as this has lately done . . ." Another letter told that often he had to revise ideas that he had thought he had proved. He added, "If there is no other use discovered of electricity, this, however, is something considerable, that it may help to make a vain man humble."

Friends asked him, "Why such a fuss about this electricity —a childish amusement! What is it good for?"

Franklin did not mind the question; it was one he often asked himself. Then he had an idea. The weather was fine. He invited a few good friends to a picnic on the wooded bank of the Schuylkill River. Hampers of Deborah's good food and a live turkey promised well for the dinner.

To the astonishment of his guests, Franklin killed the turkey with an electric spark and then, with another, lighted the fire to roast it.

"You see," he said, laughing. "Electricity has a practical use." The picnic was a success.

Franklin now began to explore the qualities of electricity. His experiments proved that electricity is both positive and negative, that glass is a non-conductor; and, by an ingenious use of two wires and a cork, he showed electricity as a current and led the way toward making a battery.

These experiments were reported in letters to Mr. Collinson, who, in 1751, published the material as a book, *Experiments and Observations on Electricity*. This book was read in Europe and gave Franklin a fine reputation. Men who, unknown to Franklin, had done similar experiments were glad to have their work confirmed; others were led on to even more advances.

In his letters, Franklin gave new use to more than a score of words that other scholars soon adopted. Among these are armature, battery brush, charging, condenser, electric shock, electrify.

All this while Franklin pondered the question—are electricity and lightning related? One day he asked a Junto member.

"Don't be foolish, Ben! You know as well as I do that lightning is simply an explosion of nauseous gas!"

"That's the accepted theory," Ben agreed. "But theory can be wrong." The friend shook his head. And Franklin had no proof.

But he jotted down facts he thought lightning and electricity had in common: both have color and give out light; move swiftly; crackle on exploding; are conducted by metals; can kill animals; melt metals; leap from point to point; go through water or ice; set materials on fire. Often an electrical storm destroyed valuable buildings.

"If lightning is electricity," Franklin said, as they experimented, "perhaps a metal point on top of a building might catch it and a wire lead it into the ground—without setting a house afire."

"But *is* lightning electricity?" That must be proved.

Ben wrote Mr. Collinson suggesting that a pointed rod

might be set on a hill. If it caught electricity in lightning, wouldn't that prove them the same?

This experiment, following his directions exactly, was made near Paris in May of 1752. Sparks crackled and electricity was drawn from clouds into a jar. A few days later the king of France drove out to see the experiment repeated in another storm. But Franklin knew nothing of this for many months. So he worked out proof of another sort.

One August day that same year, Ben Franklin took his best silk handkerchief to his workshop and made a kite. He fastened sharp pointed wires at each angle of the frame, attached a tail, and tied on a sturdy, light cord. Then he called his son, who, at twenty-two, paid no attention to his father's odd activities.

William amiably agreed to help carry jars to the cowshed on a low hill in the meadow. Silly business, he thought to himself, but luckily a storm is coming, so no one is likely to notice what Father is doing.

Ben carried his kite. At the shed door he took a key from his pocket and slipped it on the cord. Thunder rumbled as he quickly got the kite high in the air.

"It's no good, is it, Father?" William said, as nothing happened.

Ben did not answer—William should know he'd not give up with just one cloud. The sky darkened. Rain poured down. Father and son stood at the door of the shed, waiting . . .

"William. *Look!*"

William glanced at his father—the man was staring, fascinated, as the fibers of the wet cord stiffened and stood erect.

His face radiant, Franklin touched the key with his knuckle—
and got a shock.

"It's electricity!" he cried out, nursing his hand. "It's
the same force we get by rubbing the glass!"

William, excited now that something was happening,
grabbed the Leyden jar; Franklin guided the current and stored
it safely. At that moment the heavens seemed to open and tor-
rents of rain poured in at the door and through the old roof,
drenching the two men.

"Let it rain!" Franklin shouted in exultation. "We've our
proof stored right in that jar! Lightning and electricity are the
same forces!"

Ben's World Widens

Before word of Franklin's kite experiment reached London, a letter from Paris came to him in Philadelphia. He read it joyfully.

"The experiment you planned was successful," it said. "You have proved beyond a doubt that lightning is electricity. We repeated the test you planned so the king could see the results. He was much pleased."

Soon an official document from the king of France arrived; Franklin was awarded an honor for his discovery. Other letters announced that he was elected to various honor societies in Europe.

The little volume of letters that Peter Collinson had published was now translated into German, French, and Latin, and quickly became a best seller. Franklin's writing was praised for clearness; his research for originality; his character for modesty. Within a few weeks, the name "Benjamin Franklin" became widely known. The report of his kite experiment added to his fame but did not create it.

Would you live with ease,
do what you ought,
and not what you please.

In the colonies word of that kite got around about the time that letters from Europe told of honors there. Colonials could hardly believe that one of their own men was famous. Soon Harvard, and Yale too, awarded honorary degrees to the candle-maker's son.

Franklin took acclaim calmly. He would have enjoyed talking with Mr. Logan about it, but this friend had died the year before. Ben missed him. But his thoughts looked ahead; he had a new project.

For seven years Franklin had studied electricity. He had excited it by friction, felt it on glittering, cold nights, drawn it from the clouds. He had studied electric eels, magnets, vacuums. And in every experiment he had tried to find some way to make electricity useful to mankind. His picnic tricks had been amusing, but he sought for something really useful.

Since boyhood he had seen misery caused by fires and had puzzled about how such disaster could be avoided. In April, before his kite experiment, he had published an article in the *Gazette* about fire insurance. The idea of insurance was not entirely new; ships had been insured in England for more than a century. His idea was new, though, as it applied to buildings.

The *Gazette* article had suggested a practical plan for an insurance company. This project was successful, so Franklin continued the idea with insurance for crops, for old age, and a sort of life insurance to help widows. All these plans were based on the ideal that men should help each other.

After his kite experiment he had a new idea; why not *prevent* fires from lightning? If electricity leaped from a cloud to his wired kite, would it not leap to a wire on a building? He experimented and found that it did. In *Poor Richard* for 1753, he printed directions for installing a lightning rod:

"Provide a small iron rod . . . of the sort used by nailers . . . one end being three or four feet in the moist ground, the other may be six or eight feet above the highest point of the building. To the upper end of the rod fasten a foot of brass wire, the size of a common knitting needle, sharpened to a fine point . . ." This point, he explained, would attract lightning and conduct it harmlessly into the ground. Ships could get protection by such a rod on top a mast with a wire dropped into the water.

Soon lightning rods began to be seen on colonial houses. England adopted the idea, and a little later, rods were used in France. Franklin did not patent this idea. His aim was to increase scientific knowledge and to help fellowmen. All his inventions were given freely to the public.

As the year 1753 came, so many demands intruded upon Franklin that he did less of the scientific work he loved. The postmaster job grew with the city and its commerce; no longer could business be done in a corner of David Hall's print shop. Ben rented a place on Market Street where Deborah helped him sort and send off mail.

As they worked, one day, Ben remarked to her, "People think that because I am no longer working steadily at the shop I have nothing to do! They lay hold of me for their purposes, imposing duties!" Counting up, they saw that he was justice of the peace, alderman, committeeman to select a site for a bridge, city councilman, and member of the assembly.

"This last is good, Debbie," he admitted. "For fifteen years I sat there, listening. Now I may have some influence."

The winter following the kite experiment, Franklin wrote many letters to Europe and received countless replies; he was considered a leading scientist. He did other writing, too; for newspapers, letters to his family and to learned men in the colonies. He especially wanted members for the philosophical society. All these letters moved slowly to their destinations because of poor postal service. As spring came on, he talked with David Hall about this matter.

"We could have better postal service, David, if we worked for it. Did I tell you that I have applied for the office of postmaster general when there is a vacancy?"

"No, you didn't, Ben. Think you could improve matters?"

"Yes. I'm so sure that I'm going to take a trip soon; inspect routes, and see how to speed the service. If you want an article for the *Gazette*, let me know. I'll be off, come better weather."

For ten weeks of that summer, Franklin rode postroads east and north. He had no authority, not yet. But by the time he got to Boston, his notebook bulged with ideas.

He had just returned from the long journey when the governor appointed him, along with Isaac Norris, speaker of the assembly, to visit Indians in Carlisle, west of Lancaster. The object was to make sure they continued loyal to the English. The need for this move did not surprise Franklin. On his journey he had heard that the French were active; they promoted friendship with Indians, and planned to block the English, north, west, and south. Ben accepted willingly, though the journey meant four days of hard traveling, each way.

At Carlisle, while they waited for the Indians and the thirty-wagon train of gifts, they met three men they needed to know: George Croghan, a half-breed trader, Conrad Weiser, a Pennsylvanian and interpreter, and Andy Montour, just returned from a conference in Virginia. Through these men, the two delegates heard news of Governor Dinwiddie of Virginia and of a promising young colonial officer, George Washington.

"We welcome your advice," Franklin assured the woodsmen. "Our aim is to strengthen Indian friendship and loyalty."

"Then I beg of you," Weiser urged, "give out no rum before talks. Promise it for later if you must, but not a drop before business."

Norris and Franklin followed this advice. The wagon train came; gifts, including guns, were handed out. After the conference, a treaty was signed—Franklin's first work in diplomacy. The Indians, in such numbers, fascinated him. He studied their dark faces and brilliant eyes, and later wrote one of his best essays about them.

Just as they got home, their mission successful, Franklin's appointment as deputy postmaster for America arrived from London. The postmaster had died, and the king divided the office, giving Franklin the north and William Hunter of Virginia the south. The salary was six hundred pounds a year, divided, "Provided the service makes that much profit"—it never had.

Now Franklin was glad that he had made the summer journey. With winter near, he needed to start improvements at once.

Postal service in the new world had begun very casually. The captain of an arriving ship handed letters to departing passengers, hoping that somehow mail would be passed on. Travelers overland carried mail and left it with the nearest innkeeper, who passed letters on to other travelers. Mail was delayed for months; often it was never delivered. Years passed before any post office was set up; more years before regular riders began work. But by 1753, there were some regular routes, though all mail was slow—three weeks from Boston to Philadelphia. In the south, service was worse.

Franklin appointed his son William to attend to details. He used his own money to start work on roads, and Deborah helped him in the office.

As the year 1754 came in, he remarked to her, "You should stay at home tomorrow, Debbie. This year I have two birthdays, and I want both of them celebrated."

"*Two* birthdays! Listen to the man! How do you figure that, Ben?"

"Easy enough! I was born on the 6th of January. With the new Gregorian calendar that day is the 17th—I celebrate both."

"Oh, that!" Deborah said. "You talked about that before. Why did they have to mess up the calendar?"

"They didn't. They straightened it out. Our year now begins in January, and we count days the same way they do in Europe. But to do this, we had to drop eleven days, beginning last September. Mind now, Debbie—two birthdays!"

Almanacs were issued early that year so anniversaries could be planned correctly. In Virginia, Major George Washington celebrated his day on the 22nd of February instead of the 11th. And a lad named Thomas Jefferson had his on April 13th. For a time there was confusion; then people became used to the new way.

Improvement in post service began barely in time. In the spring of 1754, the colonies felt a need for closer ties. France, the enemy of England, controlled the St. Lawrence and was building a line of forts to connect this area with her possessions on the Mississippi and the Gulf. English colonies would then be surrounded.

Governors of several northern colonies arranged a conference with the Indians at Albany, in June, to see if they could check the French. Franklin was one of four Pennsylvania delegates appointed to attend. He was so stirred by the need for united action that he wrote an article on the subject for the *Gazette* and printed with it one of his small drawings. He pictured a snake, broken in pieces, each marked with an initial of a colony—P for Pennsylvania, NY for New York. Underneath were the words: Join or Die.

"Never saw a picture of a political idea," readers remarked. "Trust Ben to think of something new!"

"But how can colonies join?" No one knew the answer.

Delegates left for Albany on the 3rd of June. Speaker Norris, John Penn, grandson of the founder, Richard Peters, secretary of the colony, and Franklin rode in a coach. Several assistants, one William Franklin, followed on horseback. When about to leave, Norris set his Poor Richard Almanac on his knee and wrote their names, the date, the hour—10 A.M.—and the destination.

"I couldn't do without my almanac, Ben," Norris said. "I like your new idea of putting in blank pages for my own records."

Franklin glanced at the book; this year's cover was green with dark red flowers; he saw pages filled with weather reports, family news, and "Chimneys cleaned"—all in Norris's small neat writing.

On the journey, the delegates discussed the conference, and the real need for union. How could it be brought about?

"Surely you have an idea, Ben," Peters said. "You wrote about it."

"It seems clear that each province must be independent to manage internal affairs," Ben replied. "But we should unite for defense. United, with one purse, one leader, one plan, we would be strong. The leader, a president-general, appointed by the king, would be aided by a grand council, appointed by the assemblies, and meeting annually. From the council, seven members and the president-general could be on call for emergencies."

"Each independent for its own business," Norris nodded, agreeing. They discussed the matter every day of the journey. On the 17th they reached Albany—and that was set down in the almanac, too.

The Dutch town overflowed with delegates, clerks, and Indians from the Six Nations confederation. Gifts were presented; long, tedious meetings with the many chiefs were endured. It was soon plain that the French had caught the interest of the Indians, traditional friends of the English. Safety required that the mother country and her colonies act in unison.

Franklin's plan got favorable comment, and a committee was appointed to consider it and present it to all colonies. Results from this would be slow. Franklin wondered—was it already too late? Washington and his brave Virginians had been defeated at Fort Necessity. The French already had forts and Indian allies.

Months passed after the delegates returned home. Franklin's plan was rejected by one colony after another.

"It gives too much power to the king and other colonies!"

"Too democratic!" England said, also rejecting it.

As a dream of union faded, England refused to give protection to new settlers. Families, such as Franklin had seen moving westward, in wagons or on horseback, faced wilderness and Indians alone. The ignorance of the English about the new world was incredible.

In the spring of 1755, war came—outright war with France that England could not ignore. All colonies were threatened; Virginia and Pennsylvania were near disaster. Virginia had been dealt a hard blow. Pennsylvania Quakers would not help arm, and by law the vast Penn lands could not be taxed even for defense. When General Braddock and his troops landed in Virginia, Pennsylvania declined to help build a road for his advance west.

"The general is fighting mad," a messenger from Braddock said to the governor. "He hates Pennsylvanians worse'n the French!"

Ben Franklin was rushed off to make peace. With him were the governors of Massachusetts and New York, William Franklin, and others. The journey was agreeable, and Franklin needed but a week to make Braddock understand Pennsylvania's loyalty —and difficulties. He was about to leave when a messenger reported to Braddock that no wagons were to be had.

"You need wagons, General?" Franklin asked innocently.

"Of course!" Braddock snapped. "I need two hundred!"

"I doubt if there are twenty-five around here. It's a pity you didn't come to Philadelphia. Many of our farmers have wagons."

"Then get them for me! Write your own terms—but get wagons." He hardly glanced at the contract Franklin wrote.

Franklin and William left at once on their mission. They stopped at each Pennsylvania farm they passed, and Franklin made clear the terms: a wagon and four horses and a driver, fifteen shillings daily; packhorse with saddle, two shillings, without saddle, eighteen pence. Pay to begin on joining Braddock's army. Franklin always added, "If you don't join, Braddock may take your horses anyway."

"How do we know he'll pay?" some asked bitterly.

"I carry seven hundred pounds the general entrusted with me," Ben told them. "I'll pay from my own pocket if that is not enough."

In twenty days he had one hundred and fifty four-horse wagons at the camp, along with two hundred and fifty-nine pack-horses and quantities of feed. Braddock was delighted.

"I beg of you, Mr. Franklin, stay and manage my supplies."

Franklin stayed a while. He found that British officers, who had to buy their own food and supplies, lacked many things.

He sent William home. Soon the young man returned with twenty packhorses laden with sugar, tea, coffee, chocolate, and other things—a gift from Philadelphians (including Franklin). Braddock's hatred of Pennsylvanians vanished.

On the day the army moved toward Fort Duquesne, Braddock bade Franklin a reluctant farewell. "I'll see you later," he said. "We'll take forts on up to Niagara and then return."

"The wilderness way is long and hard," Franklin warned. "And I beg of you, beware of Indian surprises."

"You are thinking of colonial troops," Braddock said loftily. "My men are trained. We will not be surprised."

Colonel Washington, now acting as volunteer aide on Braddock's staff, stood near. He and Franklin exchanged a meaningful glance that told of shared knowledge of Indian dangers. But to speak frankly to a British general was out of the question.

At home, Franklin forwarded supplies bought with his own money. Braddock sent back an order for one thousand pounds, two-thirds of what had been spent—and then no more came— just dreadful news!

Near night, breathless, exhausted riders galloped in, shouting, "Braddock is defeated!" "All is lost!" People gathered in crowds to hear the incredible news.

"It was a surprise attack near the fort!"

"Ten minutes, and the dead filled the woods! We didn't have a chance!"

For days, more men staggered in. Braddock, mortally wounded, had died. Washington, two horses killed under him, led the retreat and saved lives when all seemed doomed. Citizens hardly listened to further tales, being absorbed with their own dangers.

No one had dreamed that Braddock would *fail!* If the British troops could not save themselves—who, now, would save Philadelphia? Only the wilderness lay between the city and the enemy—and Indians did not fear the wilderness.

"General" Franklin

During the autumn after Braddock's defeat, Indian raids wiped out whole settlements north and west of Philadelphia. When Franklin had gone to Carlisle, he had seen many of these brave pioneers traveling westward in their Conestoga wagons. Now hundreds of them were dead—slaughtered cruelly.

"What shall we *do?*" frightened city people asked themselves.

"Colonel Dunbar should push the Indians back!"

But Dunbar and the small remnant of the king's army were comfortable in Philadelphia, and there they intended to stay.

Need for action stirred the bitter quarrel between the assembly and the governor.

"We have to have money to raise an army," assemblymen said.

"You dare not tax the Penn lands," the governor reminded them. These lands, given William Penn by King Charles II in

Good sense is a thing
all need, few have,
and none think they want.

1681, included 26 million acres of the best land in the colony.

Taxation was not the only problem. Many thought Quakers were not sincere, were even cowards.

"Why should we fight for men who will not help defend us?" many citizens asked. The good influence of William Penn's religion seemed lost in bitterness. Franklin tried to make friends in England understand the trouble—without success.

But when Indians attacked a settlement just north of the city, people were badly frightened. Money was voted; Franklin's bill for defense passed quickly, its preamble legally exempting Quakers from military service hardly noticed.

Franklin wrote a fictional article for the *Gazette;* a dialogue between X, Y, and Z, arguing the right to hold religious scruples against army service. Most readers understood this better than sermons and, at least for the time, accepted the situation. Men began to enlist, and supplies were gathered. In December, the governor sent for Franklin.

"We now have five hundred and forty volunteers," he said. "You are to lead the expedition north." Franklin was astonished.

"I am no military man," he said. "I know nothing of that art."

"You have sense, and men trust you. Do not argue; go at once."

So, in the worst possible month, in cold and sleet and snow, the little army marched north. William, who had run away to fight in New England a few years earlier, was Franklin's aide-de-camp and the only man in the army who'd had military experience.

Remembering Braddock's defeat, Franklin guarded against surprise. Scouts went ahead, on each side, and in the rear. Settlers passed on the way were given arms, but in the terrible weather powder was often useless. Had Indians guessed true conditions, the army would have been wiped out.

Franklin planned three forts in the Lancaster area. Work on the first began promptly. Soldiers dug a three-foot trench, cut and stripped trees, and set the pointed posts close together. That fort was finished in five days; a flag was raised, a guard set, and the army moved to the next site.

The 17th of January, 1756, Franklin's fiftieth birthday by the new calendar, was spent huddled in a rude shelter, scant protection from sleet and wind. He did not look like a world-renowned scientist! His homespun coat and cap were soaked. His face was red with cold; his shoulders, strong from hours of swimming, gave him the look of an athlete. His clear gray eyes were undaunted and his lips a thin line of determination. The men called him "General"—and felt safe where there was no safety.

The forts were barely finished when a messenger arrived, ordering Franklin back to the city. He was needed there.

"But I am needed here," he said, dismayed.

"A Colonel William Clapham happens to be living near," William said. "He served with me in New England and is looking around camp now. Maybe he'd enlist and take over." Clapham was found and accepted the responsibility, so Franklin left with the messenger.

But the governor did not send for Franklin for assembly work as he had supposed. He wanted another army raised to take Fort Duquesne. That was too much even for Ben.

"I'm not a military man," he reminded the governor. "I'll help raise troops, but they need a trained leader, not me!"

Twelve hundred men enlisted—and elected Franklin their colonel. They got up a parade in his honor; nothing like it had ever been seen in Philadelphia. They fired a salute in front of Franklin's house—an honor never given a governor or a Penn.

"And look, Debbie," Franklin said when the noise ended, "vibrations from the guns broke some of my best electrical equipment and shattered eleven of our windows."

Franklin was firm, though; he stayed in the city and worked hard to get the governor and the assembly to co-operate. For a time, it seemed that he was successful. Indians were quiet.

When the assembly adjourned for the summer, Franklin left to inspect the postal service. He had made newspapers a source of revenue; subscribers paid ninepence a year if they lived within fifty miles, and riders carried all newspapers, not just those published by the postmaster.

When Franklin got home after three months away, he found that a new governor had come and a great banquet was being planned. The party was the talk of the town. Franklin was presented with a handsome medal—awarded by the Royal Society, not, as the governor implied, by the king.

Franklin enjoyed the banquet, but he did not change his mind about the need for taxing Penn acres. The governor turned against him—no surprise to Ben. He had seen through the whole business.

In December—a year after the forts were built—Indians again attacked; governor and assembly still quarreled. It seemed like a horrid nightmare, over and over.

Unexpectedly the assembly appointed Speaker Norris and Franklin as agents to go to London to get help. Norris pleaded age and illness. Franklin, too, tried to decline.

"I'm no diplomat," he said. "I'm a printer."

"How about Carlisle and Albany?" the governor demanded. "Not a man in the colony understands people so well!"

In the end, Franklin had to agree to go and do his best. Deborah was shocked when she heard the news.

"Of course you and Sally will go with me," Ben told her.

"That we will not!" Deborah said. "Trust ourselves to a

tub of a ship? Never." Then she saw his stricken face. "You will not be gone long, Pappy," she comforted him. "You will bring them around before they know it. Anyway, Sally is too young."

Franklin looked at his twelve-year-old daughter—a pretty girl, bright and quick, always ready to fetch his slippers or wash his glass equipment. She was his pride and joy. Perhaps Deborah was right. What would Sally, or Deborah herself for that matter, do in London? And if they were unhappy, could he do his government work with wholehearted enthusiasm? He should get off quickly, do the job and return.

But there were endless delays. Lord Loudon came from New York to make a final—and useless—effort to uphold the governor. His stay caused Ben to miss the fast packet on which he had engaged passage for himself and William. They went to New York and there waited eleven weeks before Loudon let their ship depart.

Once on the way, Franklin put aside responsibilities and made a study of the little ship—its hull, masts, sails, and manner of stowing away the cargo. He suggested a change in this last that improved their speed.

Cornwall was looking its best when the Franklins landed at Falmouth. They hired a coach for the drive to London, stopping only to visit Stonehenge and Salisbury Cathedral, and arriving in London late in July of 1757.

Mr. Collinson had invited them to stay at his home, and the next several days were a continuous round of welcoming parties. Members of the Royal Society and other notables called to greet the great philosopher from America. Letters came from France, Germany, Holland, and Spain, welcoming Franklin to the old world. He saw that he must have quiet to do the work for his country, so he looked for a place to live.

"We couldn't be more fortunate!" he told William as they moved to Number 7 Craven Street. "Mrs. Stevenson is an admirable woman and promises to give us good care. Her little daughter Polly will comfort us in Sally's absence."

"Will you have enough room, Father?" William wondered.

"Plenty. She rents me the second floor—the front room for my work is large and light with our bedrooms behind and rooms on the third floor for two servants who will do for us. We shall be comfortable."

William entered the Middle Temple to study law; Franklin rented a modest little "chariot," so the representative of Pennsylvania need not go about in a dingy hack. And then he plunged into the work he had come to do.

His first business was to call upon the Penns and present the case for the colonists. The brothers were cold and formal. When he had finished they said, "No!" in one breath.

"What is that in your hand?" one asked coldly, pointing to a bit of paper Franklin held.

"Just my notes." Franklin handed it over as Penn reached for it imperatively.

"It is not dated and signed!" he cried angrily. "It is not even respectful to us."

"Make out a respectful document that we can consider formally," the other brother ordered.

"But, sir," protested Franklin, "I have no authority to write a formal document. I came to present our point of view."

"It is a pity Pennsylvania sent a man with such limited powers," the older Penn said, turning away. Franklin, dismissed, saw they would do nothing for the colony—nothing.

On his way back to Craven Street, his head ached. He was barely able to climb the stairs and take to his bed. Months of delay, anxiety, bad weather, and now this defeat were too much even for his strength. He was seriously ill for weeks. Except for the good care given by Mrs. Stevenson and Polly, Pennsylvania might have lost her diplomat.

When Franklin finally began to improve, he planned a new campaign; he would call on William Pitt, the prime minister. But colonials were held in such low esteem that he was refused an interview. The minister was planning war on the continent and had no time—not even for a member of the Royal Society.

Months passed. In two years no progress had been made toward what Franklin had supposed could be speedily settled.

William, now a barrister, wrote a five-hundred-page history of the whole Penn-colonial quarrel. He and his father between them had served the assembly for many years; their recollections made an accurate history. Franklin had it published, and the work attracted favorable comment—but no official notice.

Franklin built an electrical machine strong enough to produce a nine-inch spark—men of science flocked to his rooms to see it and to talk with the inventor. In a lighter vein, he made an Armonica—a musical instrument he had planned earlier. In a wooden cabinet, bell-like bowls of glass of different sizes

were set sidewise on a rod and turned by a treadle. When stroked
with wet fingers, they made sweet sounds very pleasing to the
ear. English friends were enchanted with his music; he had
skill playing the guitar, violin, and harp, too, and evenings with
music were popular. But no one had the slightest interest in
Pennsylvania.

Summers, the father and son traveled. They found the
house at Ecton where Uncle Benjamin had lived. They went
to Scotland where, at the University of St. Andrews, Benjamin
Franklin was given an honorary degree with the title of Doctor.

The word seemed to fit him. Colonel, General, Postmaster—those were jobs. "Doctor" represented achievement. Later, the University of Edinburgh also honored him.

All this time Franklin deeply missed his home—but he would not give up and leave until he had gained at least something for Pennsylvania. The homesickness was so great that from Scotland he sent boxes of gifts to assure Deborah and Sally of his love and remembrance. The gifts included china fruit plates with a design of melons and leaves, carpeting, tablecloths, yard goods for dresses, new-style salt spoons and a little tool for coring an apple without cutting it up—a fine novelty, he thought.

"They'll have the house full when they unpack all this," he said to William, and wished he could go with the boxes.

The countless inconveniences of London stirred Dr. Franklin's passion for improvement. Those smoky street lamps—he soon found a better way to make them—but did the Londoners want to change? No. How different from Americans—especially from Ben Franklin, who, after the lamp study, turned to experiments in ventilation.

During this time, Franklin continually tried to make people understand the problems of his colony and the Penns. He wrote, he talked, he conferred—with no visible results.

At home, affairs were in a sad state. The assembly passed several important bills, and the king let them lie on his desk. One authorized raising 100,000 pounds sterling by a tax on *all* land—a blow to the Penns if signed; to the colony if unsigned.

For the assembly, counting on Franklin's influence, had not only passed that bill taxing all land in Pennsylvania, unsurveyed wilderness land along with surveyed land—which included the Penns' twenty-six million acres. They had persuaded Governor Denny to defy the Penns, sign the bill, and send it along with other bills to London. Then, while it lay on the king's desk, they began to spend the money.

But the king did not sign. This defeat might have crushed any but a Ben Franklin; instead, it spurred him to a bold move, a compromise. Statesmen were shocked. One did not ask to compromise with a king! How little they knew Franklin. In his quiet way he suggested that surveyed land be taxed, unsurveyed, exempted.

"They are so ignorant of America," Franklin said to William, as he made his plans, "they have no idea whether or not Penn land is surveyed." The lords were won over by Franklin's suggestion; the king was pleased because he was weary of the dispute. The substitute bill was passed, a great victory.

Suddenly Franklin longed to go home. Mrs. Read, Deborah's mother, had died; she had lived with the Franklins and was much loved. Sally was older; her father wanted to see her. Postal matters did well under his long range direction, but he had new ideas he wished to undertake for the service. Three years was a long time away.

A Voice for America

The year 1760 was an important time for England. In late October, King George II died, and his grandson, George III, was crowned with ceremonies that were the talk of the land. That same year a poor instrument-maker, James Watt, began tinkering with a thing he called a steam engine. And Richard Arkwright gave up his trade of barber to do experiments that led him to making a spinning-jenny. Only the neighbors noticed these men. George III was hailed in Europe and in America.

The new king was a man of good intentions, but dull. He liked the comfort of peace. Articles urging peace flooded the press.

Franklin did not favor peace at too high a sacrifice. He wanted differences settled fairly, so that real peace could be enjoyed in the new world as well as in the old. It was no time for the agent from Pennsylvania to go home; he must make the acquaintance of the new prime minister and the head of the cab-

Would you persuade,
speak of interest,
not of reason.

inet. He must try to make clear, if anyone could, the wishes of loyal Englishmen in America.

At this time, almost all colonists thought of themselves as Englishmen. Franklin dreamed of a great empire, united in working for the good of king and countrymen. He wrote much in this vein—both humorous and serious essays.

"That man Franklin thinks England, not France, should have Canada," readers observed. "He makes a good case, too."

"He is the ablest writer we have on that viewpoint," Edmund Burke said frankly. "He sees the whole issue, and he is widely read."

But the time came when personal and post-office matters impelled Franklin's return home. Because of war he must wait for a convoy of ships; it was nearly fall of 1762 before he sailed westward. The voyage was a curious one. Weather was good, the seas smooth. Dinner parties were given on various ships in the convoy, and guests rowed back and forth for social events. At Madeira Island travelers went ashore; fresh fruits, especially fine grapes, were brought aboard.

"I hang my grapes from the ceiling," Franklin remarked. "It keeps them from crushing." The word spread from ship to ship, and cabin ceilings looked like arbors—until the fruit was eaten.

Oil was taken on at Madeira, too, and Franklin got an idea for a lamp to replace candles that dripped and sputtered in every breeze. He filled an ordinary glass tumbler one third with water and a second third with oil. He contrived a cork float and a bit of twine for a wick. The empty upper third protected the flame from breezes. The lamp gave good light for an evening of talk or games.

William was not with his father on this voyage; he stayed to court Miss Elizabeth Downes, a well-born young lady from the West Indies. And Dr. Franklin had reason to believe that by the time of William's marriage, his promised appointment as governor of New Jersey—a compliment to both father and son—would be made public.

The voyage of nine weeks ended with a joyous welcome. Franklin wrote to a friend:

> "On the first of November I arrived safe and well at my own home after an absence of near six years, found my wife and daughter well; the latter grown quite a woman with many amiable accomplishments acquired in my absence; and my friends as hearty and affectionate as ever with whom my house was filled for many days, to congratulate me on my return. . . ."

He had been re-elected to represent Philadelphia in the assembly; when that body convened, they voted him salary and expenses for his stay in England.

In February, William and his bride arrived, and after being entertained in the city, were escorted to their new home at the capital of New Jersey. The season was a happy one.

Then Dr. Franklin settled down to his old routine: the assembly, writings, and, in the summer, a sixteen-hundred-mile journey on postal inspection. Sally went with him for the part of the trip north of New York, and he found her good company and was proud to introduce her to relatives and friends in Boston. He wrote to Deborah:

"Sally keeps to her horse the greatest part of the journey. . . ." He added, "I approve of your opening all my English letters as it must give you pleasure to see that people who knew me there so long and so intimately, retain so sincere a regard for me."

The improvements made after this trip allowed postriders to travel by night as well as day, speeding the service.

Benjamin Franklin was now fifty-seven years old; he looked forward to building a new and larger home where he could entertain comfortably, and to devoting his time to study and writing. That work on the Art of Virtue, planned so long ago, was not yet begun. But fate had other plans for him.

England and France made formal peace in February of 1763.

Unfortunately, Indians did not know about names signed on a paper in Paris, nor would they have been impressed if told. For years they had been stirred to war by both English and French; Indians did not turn off hate at the signing of a paper. And of all the colonies, Pennsylvania suffered most.

"If we could rid ourselves of the Penns," some said, "if we could be united, we could manage our affairs."

Others supported the Penns loyally.

"We need a charter from the king, like other colonies," was said.

It was a time of strife and raids. Churches in the city took up collections. Christ Church raised nearly 700 pounds and sent a missionary to distribute among needy settlers the food and clothing that money bought. It was not the time for a middle-aged philosopher to take even a well-earned rest.

In the autumn a new governor came—no man stayed long in that post. John Penn, of the original family, had come and was cordially welcomed. Surely with a Penn as governor all would now be well.

Instead matters grew worse. Hotheaded settlers up Lancaster way murdered a whole village of peaceful Indians. Other friendly Indians fled to Philadelphia for safety. The governor, hearing that Indians had come, hid in Dr. Franklin's house while Franklin and three others rode out to Germantown, faced the irate settlers, and persuaded them to let peaceful Indians live.

When the immediate emergency was over, Franklin wrote a pamphlet on justice between the races. In part it said:

> "If an Indian injures me, does it follow that I may revenge that injury on all Indians? It is well known, that Indians are of different tribes, nations and languages . . . If the French, who are white people, should injure the Dutch, are they to revenge it on the English, because they too are white people? The only crime of these poor wretches seems to have been, that they had a reddish-brown skin, and black hair; and some people of that sort, it seems, had murdered some of our relations. If it be right to kill men for such a reason, then, should any man, with a freckled face and red hair, kill a wife or child of mine, it would be right for me to revenge it, by killing all the freckled, red-haired men, women and children, I could afterwards anywhere meet with."

He printed it at his own expense and gave copies to all who could read. It did seem to have some effect, at least for a while.

But the governor hated Franklin as a man hates one whose courage exposes his own cowardice. He vetoed two bills Franklin had written: one to allow volunteer soldiers to have a voice in choosing their officers; the other to tax Penn lands.

"We need to be a royal province like Virginia and Massachusetts," a friend said to a group who were gathered in Franklin's home.

"Write a petition direct to the king, Ben. Surely if we appeal to him we can have justice."

So Ben wrote. More than 3,000 citizens signed that paper.

Instead of help, word came of a new tax—Grenville's Stamp Tax it was called—and its purpose was to fill the nearly empty royal chest. The colonial agents then in London were shocked, even though Grenville pretended friendly consideration.

"We propose to tax all papers, and I have called you to explain our method. If you think of a better way to raise the same money, now is the time to tell me your suggestion," Grenville said.

"What could we answer?" the worried agents wrote home. "Grenville knows all the colonies are in debt. He knows the new tax will be set by parliament, not by our own assemblies as we have requested—and as our charters provide."

Colonists wrote protests. Grenville simply waited.

In the autumn, Franklin was defeated by twenty-five votes for his seat in the assembly; the Penn party was strong in the city. But when the assembly met, he was elected agent to go to London; the colony as a whole wanted him there.

"We need a voice for America," men said. "We can trust Ben."

This time he did not suggest that Deborah and Sally go with him. The new house on Oriana Street, between Third and Fourth, was being built. Anyway, he would not be gone long. On a bleak November day, more than three hundred friends rode with him to Chester, where he boarded the ship.

He had been at home about two years; he had worked tirelessly for peace in the colony. He still felt hopeful—if he could only make the king and his circle understand! After a quick though rough passage, he settled to this task in his rooms on Craven Street.

Agents from the other colonies came to see him—Grenville had promised them an interview in February. Preparing for this, the agents went over the Stamp Act carefully. It was a puzzling thing.

A stamp, bought from a government collector, must be put on fifty-four sorts of papers—three pence on a small legal paper; two pounds on a college diploma; two pence on an almanac; two shillings on a bail bond.

At the interview, Franklin spoke fearlessly to Grenville.

"If the king needs help, let him ask us; we are loyal citizens. But let him ask us through our assemblies, legally, not through parliament." But his protest did no good.

By midsummer, every ship brought rebellious letters to England. Patriots in Virginia and in New England were retaliating by economic boycott. Other colonies soon went along with them.

"Why doesn't Franklin *do* something?" Americans complained. "Can't he see the colonials won't endure this tax?"

"Perhaps he *does* see and waits for matters to get worse."

And matters did. Colonial agents were asked to appoint collectors; Grenville thought this a smart move. Franklin appointed his friend John Hughes. When that news came, Hughes's life was threatened. Franklin's house was mobbed. William galloped over to rescue his mother and Sally.

"Perhaps Sally'd better go," Deborah granted. "But I stay here. This is my home. Ben has done nothing wrong, that I know." And she stayed. The mob, awed by such defiance, did not touch her or her house.

The Stamp Act was to become effective November 1st. Before that date English statesmen knew that they would never collect a penny of it. English artisans and merchants rose in protest—no orders for goods came from the colonies. Englishmen were starving! The Grenville ministry fell, and a new group, more favorable to the colonies, came in. A hearing before parliament was set for February of 1766, with Dr. Franklin as a principal witness.

His turn came a few days after his sixtieth birthday. He prepared for the day with care, checking facts and figures. Witnesses stood literally "before the bar," a wooden gate arrangement which separated them from members of parliament seated on benches. Fearlessly Dr. Franklin faced the hard, set faces before him. The questions brought out facts few Englishmen knew.

"The colonies protest—have they no loyalty to the king?"

"They are loyal," Franklin answered. "They are already burdened with taxes, but they will give all they can—if the king will but ask them in the legal way, through their assemblies."

"But this money is to be spent in America . . ."

"Not where it is collected," Franklin explained. "It is meant for the conquered province of Canada—a long distance from us."

"Can't Americans afford this tax?"

"Some can. Some cannot. We are careful not to tax settlers in the wilderness. They have little or no cash and a hard life. Because of vast distances in our land, this act will work unjustly on a back-country man. If he wished to sell a bit of land, he might have to travel a month's journey to buy a stamp. The trip might cost him several pounds to buy a sixpenny stamp— is that good?" Franklin almost despaired at their ignorance of geography.

A friend of Franklin's asked for the floor.

"It is folly to alienate America!" he cried. "Each year the colonies have bought 500,000 pounds of English goods—our people count on that business. And America has 300,000 men who could fight!" Members were not impressed.

"Won't America pay anything toward war costs?"

"She will, as I have said," Franklin replied. "And she has. She has spent thousands of pounds willingly."

"That's been paid back!" someone shouted.

"Only a small part, sir," Franklin said politely. "Pennsylvania paid out 500,000 pounds and was repaid 60,000. We paid loyally, but those days are passed. American temper has changed."

Men looked startled. "What do you mean?" several demanded.

"Once a colonist's pride was to wear English-made clothes."

"And now?"

"We wear our homespun." Franklin gestured to his brown suit, woven and tailored by Deborah. "We will wear homespun

until this unjust law is repealed." There was no defiance in his firm voice as he said that word, "repealed." He simply stated a fact.

The room was hushed in heavy silence.

It is strange, Franklin thought in the stillness; Englishmen pride themselves on making any sacrifice for a principle. Yet they cannot see that men of their own sort, though living across the sea, will also sacrifice for a principle held just.

Two weeks later the hated act that could not be enforced was repealed. The boycott of goods, started by patriots in Virginia and Massachusetts, together with Franklin's voice, speaking out for America, had succeeded.

Ben celebrated by sending his wife a new gown.

In due time letters about the famous debate in parliament came to the colonies. The Reverend Whitefield had written:

> "Our worthy friend Franklin has gained immortal honor by his behavior at the bar of the House. The answer was always found equal if not superior to the questioner. He stood unappalled, gave pleasure to his friends and did honor to his country."

Philadelphians celebrated the repeal with a great parade on the king's birthday. Its main feature was a forty-foot float— built like a barge and bearing the honored name: FRANKLIN.

"I never heard so much noise," Sally wrote to her father. Others wrote too; extravagant praise crossed the ocean both ways.

Franklin enjoyed his restoration to favor. Now, he thought, my duties are done. He wrote asking the assembly's permission to return home. While he awaited a reply, a letter came from

his kinsman, Captain Timothy Folger, reporting about what
might be a strange current in the sea.

"We sailed along the edge of a different kind and movement
of water. Have you seen or experienced this, Cousin?" The
captain enclosed a rough map he had made.

Franklin was excited. He hunted through his papers and
found the map *he* had drawn on the voyage four years earlier.
The two looked very similar. With more evidence . . .

Taking fresh paper, Franklin wrote to all the ship captains
he knew, begging them to make records of temperature and
currents and send reports to him.

"Perhaps we are on the verge of something (he wrote)
which, if understood, may speed our voyages across the vast
ocean."

Ordeal in the Cockpit

The answer to Franklin's request to come home was reappointment for another year. Pennsylvania would not consider bringing home a successful agent. This meant, though, that he would have a salary and something toward his expenses. And money was giving Franklin some concern.

In September David Hall would make the last of his eighteen payments for the *Gazette*. Franklin would miss that thousand pounds a year. Fortunately the new house was built and furnished, and Deborah, though she now lived in town, did not seem to take on new or extravagant habits.

Ben's relatives were more costly to him than his immediate family. He had always been generous to sisters and brothers, nieces and nephews, and other relatives. Even in England he had two young people living with him; pretty little Sally, daughter of a distant cousin, and the lad, William Temple Franklin, William's son, whose bright attractive ways were a joy and comfort to his grandfather.

A lie stands on one leg,
truth on two.

Then came news of his own Sally; she wished to marry Richard Bache, a man of thirty, whom her father had not seen. He was a Yorkshireman; had come to New York and then to Philadelphia, where Sally met him. William disapproved, but Deborah liked Richard; Ben trusted her judgment, and gave his consent. He wrote:

> "I hope his expectations are not great of any fortune to be had with our daughter. I suppose you would agree with me that we cannot do more than fit her out handsomely with clothes and furniture, not exceeding in the whole five hundred pounds of value. For the rest, they must depend, as you and I did, on their own industry . . ."

A later ship brought word that Richard Bache had had some reverses, and Franklin hurried off a letter urging Sally to come and visit him. But she refused. The two were married in October of 1767 and lived for several years in the big new house that her father had not yet seen. Franklin buried his disappointment in political and scientific work.

For some time after the repeal of the Stamp Act, England and her colonies basked in a glow of friendship—and of lively trade. Every ship brought orders for clothing, shoes, tools, furniture, and other goods, which filled the holds of westbound ships. But as months went by, petty frictions developed.

To meet these, Georgia, then New Jersey and Massachusetts, appointed Dr. Franklin as their agent in London. He became a kind of ambassador at large for the colonies and had great prestige.

These positions paid modest salaries, together enough to relieve his money concerns. The colonies were fortunate, for no one man knew his own country so well as the postmaster. He knew most of England, too, and parts of Europe where he had vacationed. He needed this knowledge; he needed his many friends. For another bitter quarrel about taxation arose.

Grenville, still smarting about the defeat of his Stamp Act, conspired with Sir Charles Townshend, the king's treasurer, to levy a tax on all imports to America. The amount, except on tea, was to be small (at first); but it was assessed by parliament, as was the Stamp Act. Angry letters of protest came from America. Again orders for merchandise stopped. And this time conditions were not so hard, because colonial industries were developing.

English manufacturers raged. Colonists stayed firm. And tension increased.

As time brought in the 1770's, Dr. Franklin wondered whether his dream of empire ever could come about. It was a beautiful dream, he thought. Each country to have its own parliament elected by the people—England, Scotland, Ireland, Canada, and each of the thirteen colonies; with equal rights under the king who, in justice and peace, held them together—brothers across the sea.

Many a night he laid aside his pen after hours of writing and sat in thought. Was there more that he could do? And if so, what?

Not all shared Franklin's dream. Patriots in Virginia and in Massachusetts bitterly opposed Franklin as an enemy of liberty. For a time his letters made enemies on both sides of the sea. Englishmen thought he was "too America"; colonists thought he worked for the king. Few realized that he intended to try for peace as long as peace had a chance; and for time to prepare if harmony was no longer possible.

His mail was opened; there was talk of hanging him as a spy. Sea captains came to his home on Craven Street, bringing reports on the ocean currents. Franklin gave them verbal messages, knowing whom he could trust. He left no written record of some of his most important work during this period.

When British troops were sent to Boston and quartered upon the city, men saw that parliament had a special grudge against it. The citizens raged as ships delivered artillery, as troops took over the Common, the State House, and Faneuil Hall. Two years later came the shocking Boston Massacre. Boston seemed a target for trouble.

"I cannot understand why this city of all the colonies is so beset," Franklin remarked one day to a friend.

"I can explain," the gentleman said. "Many of the measures you object to are suggested by Americans themselves."

"Surely you are misinformed!" Franklin exclaimed. "I know Boston. It is my native city. My relatives live there . . ."

"I can show you proof," the friend interrupted. "But promise me that you will not divulge how you came by it!"

A few days later, he handed Franklin a packet of letters; the addresses had been removed. The letters showed they had been much read.

"Most of these were sent to William Whately," the friend

said. "It is no breach of trust to let you see them. They were meant to be read—but perhaps not by an American!"

Franklin's blood stirred as he read the clever, evil writing. Most of the letters were written by Thomas Hutchinson, governor of Massachusetts; Franklin had first known him at the Albany Conference in 1754. The letters were designed to stir up trouble for colonial patriots—with the customs, with the troops, with the citizens' normal liberties. Parliament and the king were advised to deal harshly with Massachusetts.

Franklin was angry. Hutchinson's treachery would bring war before the colonies were ready! With permission, he sent the letters to Thomas Cushing, a trusted friend in Boston, with a message of warning:

"Read, but do not publish—on your honor."

Cushing and his associates were so stirred by the unveiling of a traitor among them that they published the letters in Boston newspapers in direct violation of Franklin's trust. Later, when the newspapers got to England and Franklin's part in the business became known, a storm descended upon him.

"He stole and opened personal letters!" was said.

"He is a man without honor! A reader of private mail!"

An heir of the dead Whately sued Franklin for "profits from the sale of personal letters"—a political move planned to discredit the honest agent.

There was a storm in Boston, too. Massachusetts petitioned the king to remove Hutchinson from the governorship. This brought the affair to the Privy Council for a public hearing in the year 1774.

This council of some thirty-five members met in a famous room called the Cockpit. A huge fireplace at one end of the room made that part too hot and left the rest cold. A long table down the middle, surrounded by chairs, was for council members; others must stand during the hours of a session—including the sixty-eight-year-old Dr. Franklin. On the day of the hearing, the room was packed.

Franklin had dressed carefully for the ordeal in a flowing wig, fashionable for elderly men, and a suit of brown Manchester velvet.

"The occasion needs the support of velvet," he remarked as he left home that morning.

He stood in a niche by the fireplace, calm, composed, and with no appearance of concern.

The trial was in charge of Alexander Wedderburn, the king's solicitor-general, who was determined to make a public show of this Dr. Franklin, and discredit him for all time. He was rude, sarcastic, and cruel; his harsh words poured over Franklin, standing there by the chimney, like a flood of evil.

"Where did you get those letters?" he demanded loudly.

Franklin would not reply. He had given his promise.

"You stole them! Stole private mail!" Of course the man knew better. Franklin did not speak.

"You wrote the letters yourself! Hutchinson is known to be an honest man!" Franklin's expression did not change as more words defaming him poured forth.

No member of the council spoke to stop Wedderburn, though all of this was out of order. The council had met to consider the petition to depose Hutchinson, not to defame Franklin. The members seemed to enjoy the show Wedderburn was putting on. They applauded and at times laughed uproariously.

Dr. Franklin tried not to hear. Then suddenly words, new words, caught his attention. What was this Wedderburn saying?

"That man"—a long finger pointed at Franklin—"is plotting against England's rule in the colonies. That man wants to destroy England and create a new Republic of America."

Franklin's heart pounded with excitement though his controlled face did not move one muscle. An American Republic! He had never heard those words before. He had not consciously thought them even in the secrecy of his own mind. Yet now that they were hurled at him by the solicitor-general, he knew that they were true. He did not want an English empire. He wanted an American Republic—a nation for free men founded on justice. Such a dream was worth working for; was even worth standing silent for, under abuse—because the time for action had not yet come.

Hours later, the council meeting ended. Franklin's office of deputy postmaster of America was taken from him—without a word for his years of splendid work. Instead, as he left the room, men drew away. The famous Dr. Franklin walked out alone. Some few men, who had known Franklin well, looked shamefaced to the floor. But no one spoke to him.

On that day died the last trace of colonial-American feeling —and hope—that Ben Franklin had cherished. And he did not look back. His mind leaped forward toward a new goal. He wrote to a friend in Philadelphia:

"I wish most sincerely that a constitution was formed and settled for America, that we might know what we are and what we have . . ." This in 1774, ahead of many earnest patriots in America. But then, they had not lived in England. They could not realize that colonials were held as second-class citizens.

After his dismissal as postmaster, spies followed every move Franklin made. People at home, who ignorantly thought he was living in luxury, knew little of the truth. Tory newspapers, on both sides of the Atlantic, repeated old lies about himself and his family. Some said he was trying to set up a new state with Boston as its capital and himself as king.

Rather tiredly, he wrote articles in reply. He even dared to predict a war—an outright prediction, in print, was new.

Through it all, he longed to go home and see his family. Sally's children would be a joy. Deborah wrote feelingly:

"I wish you would come home, Pappy. I feel that if you do not come this summer, I shall never see you again." An odd idea for a sensible woman to express, he thought.

But word came that the colonies were about to hold a congress; he was told to stay on and see how that news would be received in England. Dr. Arthur Lee, one of the famous Lee brothers of Virginia, had been appointed as a substitute for Dr. Franklin. But at the moment Lee was touring in Europe. Franklin had to resign himself to stay on. And months passed.

The year 1775 was still new when a ship captain brought a personal letter. Deborah had died in December. William told of her death by a stroke and of her burial near Christ Church. Franklin's hand shook as he tried to read that letter. He thought of the time he had first seen Debbie—a pretty girl in a pink dress, standing on the steps of her parents' home as a youth walked by—a loaf under each arm, and munching a third. He had liked Deborah from that first minute. But for his trip to London by the urging of the treacherous Governor Keith they might have married sooner. Still they had had many good years together.

He looked again at the letter. William wrote:

"You had certainly better return while you are able to bear the fatigues of the voyage to a country where the people revere you and are inclined to pay attention to your opinions . . ." To him I am an old man, Franklin thought. He continued reading.

William wanted his son, Temple, to come home so he could study law at King's College in New York. "You are to bring him home with you," he wrote. And that was strange, too, for William was more Tory than many Englishmen—why not educate his son in England? William showed little knowledge of his father or his father's work. It was time to go home. Ben folded the letter and laid it aside.

But his thoughts stayed with Deborah. Without her thrift and good management he would not have been free to work for his country as he had done these many years. If we gain our freedom from England, Franklin mused, how much will be due to Deborah Franklin? Then he paused, overwhelmed by a feeling of failure. With my years of trying, I have done so little. I certainly have won no laurels that I can pass to my Debbie.

Turning from his grief, he picked up letters about the First Continental Congress and found a petition he was to present to the king—another letter! Franklin tried to deliver it in person; it seemed important to make another attempt for a peaceful solution. He had to content himself with handing it to Lord Dartmouth. Perhaps the king never saw that paper.

The congress of 1774 had adjourned to meet May 10th, 1775. Franklin stayed on in England until March, hoping vainly for some understanding with the new minister of colonial affairs. He arrived in Philadelphia May 5th, 1775, sixteen days after the battle of Lexington, where the embattled New England farmers took a hand in the making of history.

The Struggle for Freedom

During the voyage home Dr. Franklin kept careful notes about his observations of that strange and intriguing ocean current he had studied. Several times each day he tied a thermometer on a strong cord and dropped it into the water. Yes, this current they were now crossing was warmer than other parts of the ocean: it was a warm river in the sea.

"Going east," Franklin wrote, "a captain would do well to follow the current north and then east, to speed his crossing." On a map he marked it the "Gulf Stream" because it appeared to come from the Gulf of Mexico. "Strange," he thought as he read over his notes, "that no other scientist seems to have noticed this current. Perhaps they have not crossed the Atlantic as often as I have."

Finally the ship turned into the Delaware and neared home.

Twilight had come to Philadelphia when Franklin and his grandson landed and went to the house on Oriana Street. Sally

Our cause
is the cause of
all mankind . . .

welcomed them and proudly introduced her husband and children. Word of the arrival got around, and quickly the spacious rooms were filled with friends who came to welcome the travelers.

"You're looking well, Ben," one said. "Where's your wig?"

"I've given up wigs," Franklin answered. "I'm old enough to be comfortable. Why should I mind that my hair is thin and gray? I'm fat, too," he added, forestalling that comment.

"Well, fat becomes you, Ben. We'll put you to work and wear it off in no time."

"How you talk!" another laughed. "As though Ben hadn't worked hard all his life!" It was good to be called Ben; to enjoy the easy give and take of old friends.

The next morning Franklin set out early for a stroll. In his nine years away, the city had grown more than he'd realized. People looked prosperous. He saw new shops and wharves crowded with shipping. A new inn at Walnut and Fifth Street even had his name—Franklin Inn, a surprise to him.

That first morning the assembly met and voted Benjamin Franklin and two others "as deputies appointed by this house to attend the Continental Congress." Newspapers published May 10 marked his arrival with flowery poetry and prose. In a single day he was caught up in a whirl of activity, social and political.

Early delegates to the Second Continental Congress began to arrive; when the time of their coming was known, bands and committees met them outside the city. This music added a festive note to the excitement around town. When the congress opened, almost all of the sixty-three delegates were in their places.

Franklin met Thomas Jefferson and Patrick Henry. He chatted with George Washington, whom he had known in Braddock's camp. In the friendly fashion of the city, groups dined together and compared ideas and experiences.

Franklin soon saw that John Dickinson, a man of wealth and position, devoted to the Penn family—and a troublemaker for the colony—was the strong leader of the conservative faction. Likely John Adams, the patriot from Massachusetts, would be the leader against him. Franklin listened and watched as Dickinson urged another petition to the king; would they never learn? Ben almost laughed aloud when *he* was appointed on the committee to write this document!

Then the congress went on to other business. Franklin was made postmaster and ordered to plan postal routes for the united colonies. George Washington, wearing his old uniform and ready for service, was chosen general of the little army. Franklin was appointed on the committee to draft regulations for him.

In a few days Franklin was serving on ten important committees of the congress. He was also on the Committee of Safety, charged with putting Pennsylvania in a good state of defense.

Sally came downstairs sleepily one morning to find her father dressed and at the door.

"Going so early!" she exclaimed. "It's not yet six o'clock."

"Good morning, my dear," he answered cheerfully. "I'm due at the Committee of Safety in five minutes. Congress meets at nine."

"But you worked all evening, Father," Sally reproved him.

"Our country's business does not count hours, Daughter."

Quietly he closed the door and was off. It seemed that no committee was complete without Dr. Franklin. How fortunate, he
thought as he stepped along, that he now lived near the State
House.

The Continental Congress was a curious body. It had no
legal right to direct the affairs of all the colonies, yet united
direction was needed. So the people gave tacit consent to congress's decisions. This fact, perhaps more than any other, showed
that the majority of the colonists were patriots and wished to be
united. Scores of details were presented to congress, many trifling
but time absorbing; so important business, needing study, was
given to committees. Members, in the main, were men of distinction and known integrity; they carried the feeble little nation
through its difficult beginning.

In the sessions of congress, Franklin listened carefully and
spoke little, wanting to understand his countrymen's thinking.
Mr. Dickinson and his associates continually held the floor,
while patriots fumed.

"One would think congress was for the king," several
complained.

"Let them talk," Franklin advised. "Our turn will come
when their words are used up."

That day came when adjournment was being suggested.
Into a hot and weary session Franklin landed a blow—the dream
of union he had had in England. But now there was a vital
change; England was left out. Franklin proposed that the thirteen colonies join together with Ireland, Canada, the West
Indies, Bermuda, Florida, and Nova Scotia, in a union to last

until England ended her oppression or, failing that, forever.

The plan was heard in stunned silence. It was not acted on—Franklin had not expected it would be—the time was not yet ripe. But it jolted congress and gave members new thoughts to consider during the five-week recess.

During this interval, Dr. Franklin took thirteen-year-old William Temple to New Jersey to visit his father. Governor Franklin was a handsome, agreeable man, happily married and devoted to duties of his colony and home. He was a skilled farmer, too, interested in crops and stock raising.

"We are doing good work in the colonies, Father," he explained as he showed his father and his son around. "Colonel Washington and Mr. Jefferson set us a good example, though they would do better if they let politics alone!"

Dr. Franklin attempted to defend these two, but William talked so abusively against them that his father was shocked. After a few unhappy days, Dr. Franklin left for home. His grandson chose to go with him. It was hardly a surprise to hear later that the governor had been arrested for active work against the congress. Franklin realized that he could not interfere; William had chosen his course. So he tried to forget sadness in hard work.

On the 13th of September, when congress reconvened, the city was astir with military business. Forts on the Delaware were building; the saltpeter works were producing; two of six powder mills planned were at work, and a factory was completing the amazing number of twenty-five muskets a day. Postal service was improving; for a time there were two separate services, royal and colonial, both planned by Benjamin Franklin.

That fall Franklin was elected a member of the Pennsylvania Assembly but had to be excused to do even more vital work.

Shocking news had come from General Washington. The little army in Massachusetts had no shelter, no food, no fuel, no clothing, and few military supplies. Men were going home for the winter. Congress appointed a committee—Benjamin Franklin, Thomas Lynch of South Carolina, Benjamin Harrison of Virginia. Orders were, "Go to Cambridge. Confer with the general and with delegates from other colonies."

The journey took thirteen days and could have been one long parade, for people were eager to honor Dr. Franklin. But he was even more eager to get on with helping Washington.

A four-day conference with the general, his staff, and other delegates, produced a workable plan for the army. The delegates promised that congress would deal fairly with soldiers from all the colonies.

While returning, the committee heard tragic news; the port city of Falmouth (later Portland) was wantonly burned. Its people were left homeless and starving—with winter about to begin. Franklin felt a deep bitterness at this attack on civilians. Indeed, the temper of most of the colonists changed with this cruel and useless act.

While in England, Franklin had urged a young writer, Thomas Paine, to come to the colonies. Paine, now in America, sensed truly the spirit of the patriots and wrote an inspiring pamphlet entitled *Common Sense*. That pamphlet, harsh mess-

ages from the king, the burning of Falmouth, added to earlier
happenings, aroused colonists. Dickinson's followers shrank
away, and a united spirit surged through the colonies. But many
were frightened by the rapid change.

"We are not ready for war! We cannot fight England—
alone!"

"Would we be alone? Would not France—Spain—Holland
help us?" Such words were spoken in whispers.

There was even a tale of a nameless man, French, it was
said, who came to congress by night, offering aid against England.
True or false, the tale encouraged the idea of foreign aid. But
how to get that aid was a baffling problem, though it need not
have been.

Few of his countrymen realized Benjamin Franklin's ca-
pacities. He was a scientist, a member of the Royal Society. He
had taken vacations in Europe, and he knew men in many
countries. He had worked for the colonies in England. The
parades, the newspaper articles, showed this much was known
in America.

But the elderly doctor had a disarming way. At home, in
congress, on journeys, he was quiet; he never talked about himself. He looked the part of a homely, kindly old man. Few
people realized that his was one of the best minds of his century,
that among his friends were men in high places as well as sea
captains of many nations, and merchants in every important
European port.

In November, 1775, congress appointed a committee to
sound out friends in Europe; Benjamin Franklin was made

chairman because he had lived abroad. He promptly wrote many letters, among others to Professor Dumas, a native Swiss who for years had been a journalist in Holland where Franklin knew him so well that he was certain of his vigorous support of freedom. The letter was cautious—it might be opened and read en route. It begged Dumas to "sound out the mood of diplomats there; and to suggest privately to merchants that arms, gunpowder, and saltpeter were needed and brought high prices."

The same eastbound ship carried letters to Arthur Lee in London and to a Spanish prince in Madrid.

Impatient with slow communications, congress grew bolder. The committee was allowed to send an agent to France. Silas Deane of Connecticut was chosen. Deane was a handsome, likeable gentleman, graduate of Yale, lawyer, and member of the first and second congresses. He didn't speak French, but that seemed no objection. Of the dozen or more men sent abroad during this period, but one spoke French, and he, Benjamin Franklin, was the only one of the group who had not attended college.

"I am writing letters of introduction to friends in Paris," Franklin told Deane. "I want you to meet Dr. Dubourg. He knows our cause. He speaks English and will arrange a meeting with Count de Vergennes, minister of foreign affairs."

"You will write instructions for me, too," Deane begged.

"Perhaps that would be helpful," Franklin granted. He wrote many pages: Deane was to ask for uniforms, artillery, ammunition; to explain that ships were started across the sea laden with rice, tobacco, and other cargo in payment. This was all daring business. Without Franklin's knowledge of Europe it might never have been undertaken.

People hardly noticed Silas Deane's departure because they were disturbed about Canada. Word came that the American forces had failed in their attempt to take Quebec. "The army is disorganized. Smallpox, hunger, waste our forces," the message to congress said.

"We should send a committee," several suggested.

"Send Ben Franklin."

"In winter?" "Such a distance?" "The man is turning seventy!"

"Ask! He will refuse nothing for his country!"

In a few days Dr. Franklin, with Samuel Chase and Charles Carroll, both of Maryland, set off on their long, cold journey. They rode to New York, sailed up the Hudson—and were nearly destroyed by a storm—rode across country to Lake George, sailed north to the end of Lake Champlain, then traveled over land and river to Montreal. Franklin was so exhausted that he had to warm himself in bed for a few hours before he could attend the reception of welcome given for them.

A conference the next day showed that Canada was lost to the united colonies. There was no money and no army; communication and travel were slow and hard—hope was not enough. News that a British fleet had arrived at Quebec was the final blow; the colonies had no fleet. The tiny colonial army was quickly withdrawn southward, charged with the task of keeping the British north of the great river. Wisdom said: retreat, avoid further losses.

The committee was gone from Philadelphia more than ten weeks and did its best in a hopeless cause.

A couple of days after their return, Mr. Carroll called to inquire about Dr. Franklin; the cold, the hard journey, had brought on fever and gout. He found Franklin sitting up, his leg propped on a cushioned chair, reading a letter.

"I'm fine, now!" Franklin said, waving the letter. "We have a big shipment of powder—I thought it would never come!"

"Then you won't have to outfit the army with bows and arrows, as you thought in Canada," Carroll said. Franklin joined in the laugh.

"But I really meant it," he added. "Forests provide plenty of material, and the sight of flying arrows is frightening—I learned that during Indian fighting. But I'm glad for the powder."

While that committee had been in Canada, dramatic events had happened in Pennsylvania. At long last, the Penns were defeated; but during the four months following, the colony had no government at all. The people were calm. They appointed delegates to a conference which in due time arranged for delegates to a constitutional convention, where a new government was formed. The dignity and good behavior of the citizens during this period encouraged colonists to believe that men really could govern themselves.

It was no surprise to Franklin to learn that he was again on a committee—the one charged with the important duty of writing a document stating the colonies' independence. For this task congress selected the committee by ballot, choosing

Thomas Jefferson, Benjamin Franklin, John Adams, Robert
Livingston, and Roger Sherman.

Franklin had gone to the country home of a friend, to rest
and get well. The new committee rode out to meet with him.

"This is really Mr. Jefferson's committee," Franklin said
quickly, when they had explained their mission. "You, sir, have
the legal knowledge, the background of history and philosophy,
and the proved ability to write your thoughts in suitable prose.
But we shall back you up." And so it was agreed.

Mr. Jefferson worked hard for many days, and when they read the paper, the committee had few suggestions—and those trifling—to make before the paper was read in congress. Perhaps Franklin's best service came during the days of debate. Thomas Jefferson was a sensitive man; he had worked hard. He suffered miseries as his carefully chosen phrases were argued over and a few were changed. Franklin sat by him through this trying time. He comforted him with wise words, diverting stories, and somehow the time passed. The document was approved, and members gathered at the desk to sign. The signature, B. Franklin, with the flourish beneath that he had adopted, stood out boldly on the document.

Word of the signing got around, and crowds gathered. Bells rang joyously and people rejoiced when the paper was read to those gathered in the square behind the State House.

The reading over, people rushed into the State House and tore royal pictures and insignia from the walls. Others rolled barrels of tar into the open square, piled the royal tokens on top, and set fire to the pile. As black smoke rose to the sky, people shouted wildly, "Now we are free!"

Shopkeepers and private citizens rushed home. They, too, tore down the king's pictures and all signs with a royal mark, and burned the hated things in the streets.

While this was going on in Philadelphia, fast riders carried copies of the declaration to all the colonies and to General Washington, who was with his army on Long Island. On July 9th, he had the document read aloud to the troops. In spite of their danger, with the British army camped near, they were cheered by this clear statement of the cause for which they fought.

Back in the house on Oriana Street, Franklin had a letter from Dumas in Holland. It was filled with helpful suggestions, but reminded him that time was required; they must move cautiously. Dumas' letter ended, "I will devote my life to your glorious cause."

Little other news came from overseas.

All that hot summer while congress labored with military problems and the efforts to make a new government, Washington's impoverished army was in danger. It retreated north, up the Hudson. Many a patriot was plagued by questions. Had the declaration come too soon? Would the cause of freedom fail?

Dr. Franklin at Passy

Autumn came. General Washington continued his retreat. General Howe with his well-equipped army occupied New York City.

Supplies for the Americans were frighteningly scarce when Dr. Franklin received the long-awaited letter from Dr. Dubourg of Paris. He skimmed the pages hastily, then hurried over to the State House to share its contents with congress.

"He thinks France will support us?" A member who knew a little French had seized the letter.

"Read on," Franklin replied cheerfully. "No, give it to me. I can translate as I read."

Dubourg had been working, the members heard. He could get trained officers—should he send them over? If so, what should he promise them as to pay and rank? He could send a skilled man to set up a factory for making needles and pins—was it true the colonies needed these things? Everyone he had dared consult favored helping the "Thirteen United Colonies," but none agreed as to what to do.

We must all hang together,
or most assuredly,
we shall all hang separately.

"You will need engineers—I have promised free passage for two. You will need artillerists—what shall I promise them?"

"We do not know, ourselves!" exclaimed a member.

"But we do know that we need trained men to fight he British army. Get on with the reading, Ben."

" 'Our merchants will accept in payment grain, peltries, whalebone, and anything you can raise in your climate. I can get you good prices—better than England will pay—if you will speed the goods to Nantes.' " The whole letter was encouraging, but it raised more questions than it solved.

"It appears that the French prime minister knows what Dubourg is doing and has not stopped him," a member noted. "When Silas Deane arrives with official credentials, he should be welcome."

"But we should set up an imposing embassy, elected by ballot," another suggested. "We could give such men power to enter into secret business."

A few days later such a ballot was taken. Franklin, Jefferson, and Deane, because he was on the scene, were elected.

"I am old and good for nothing," the seventy-year-old Franklin remarked to the member next to him. "As the store-keeper said of his remnants, 'I am but the fag end, you may have me for what you please.' " He agreed to go despite the late autumn voyage and the danger of capture. Unfortunately, Mrs. Jefferson was ill, and Mr. Jefferson felt he could not leave her, so Arthur Lee, then in London, was elected in his place.

Before leaving, Franklin turned over the post-office business to his son-in-law, Richard Bache, and arranged to loan to congress, for its immediate needs, "all the cash he could raise"—a large sum. At the last minute he gave his files of letters and his autobiography to a friend for safekeeping.

Happily, he did not travel alone. His two grandsons, William Temple Franklin, about sixteen, and Benjamin Franklin Bache, seven, called Benny, went with him. They were to attend school near Paris.

They traveled on the swift little ship *Reprisal*. On the voyage, Franklin not only studied the Gulf Stream and winds and sky, but he thought deeply of what he might do in France. The United States, he felt sure, need not stand alone. Self interest would urge Holland, France, and Spain to help her.

Holland would like to see England's growing sea trade curtailed. France and Spain resented England's hold on the new world, and would like to get her out of the West Indies. But moves with these nations must be made slowly, discreetly.

Meanwhile, Silas Deane was meeting men Dr. Franklin knew, and others—Pierre Beaumarchais for one. He was a brilliant playwright, whose *Barber of Seville* had pleased the king.

One day, as Beaumarchais was at the palace, he spoke of the trouble between England and her colonies.

"You would do well to help America, Sire," he said boldly. "If England must fight a sturdy enemy, she will let France alone!" This idea intrigued Louis XVI. No European nation wanted more war with England; perhaps Spain would help?

Clever Beaumarchais saw a chance to help the colonies and make money. He persuaded France and Spain to loan him funds; he opened an importing house, which he named Hortalez, and bought supplies for the colonies, in secret, of course. When Silas Deane arrived, frustrated by long delay and dazed by the strange language, the activities at Hortalez were almost too much for him.

It was a relief when the *Reprisal* got Dr. Franklin to France in the record time of a month—and along with the Franklins, landed a cargo of indigo and two prizes captured near France. These, combined, more than paid the expenses of setting up an embassy for the United States.

The French people—scholars, politicians, and common folk —welcomed the famous Dr. Franklin. He was besieged with invitations and callers. In the handsome house Beaumarchais had taken, there was not a minute he could call his own. So, presently, he accepted an invitation to take part of a house in Passy, a suburb two miles out on the road to the palace at Versailles. The grandsons were put in school, and Dr. Franklin began real work.

The man Paris welcomed was quiet, almost meek; he dressed plainly and wore no wig. This at the time when statesmen were apt to be arrogant; when gentlemen wore elaborate clothes and wigs so high that hats were carried under the left arm.

"There's Dr. Franklin," men pointed him out on the street.

"Are you sure? You don't know him."

"Who else would appear without a wig? I hear he dresses his hair himself. But then he is famous; he does as he pleases."

There was soon another innovation. In the chill weather, Franklin began to wear the warm fur cap he had brought with him. This delighted his admirers. Painters begged to do his portrait, with the big cap pulled well down and comfortable. It became the mark by which he was known in Paris.

A desire for his likeness became a fad. Painters, etchers, and sculptors came to Passy asking for sittings. They took so much time that he had to call a halt if he was to do his own work. So the artists made copies of portraits already made. His likeness was used in rings, on medals and snuff boxes and other things. He

wrote to his sister Jane, "My face is almost as well known as that of the Man in the Moon."

When Arthur Lee came over from London, he could hardly endure the friendly attention paid to "that old man." But fortunately Silas Deane was proud of Dr. Franklin and worked well with him.

In the house at Passy, Franklin set up a small printing press.

"Going to run a newspaper?" Temple asked, when he came for a brief visit from school. None of the boys had presses at home.

"We might," Franklin replied. "Though it's more likely I'll use it for pamphlets and letters when I need many duplicates. I like to run a press. Want to learn?"

Temple did. Soon he was able to copy letters and set type. In all he made himself so helpful that later he left school and was secretary to his grandfather.

Dr. Franklin had many matters that needed conferences and study. He must cheer the patriots at home, worry the English, and convince the French that America would be victorious— not an easy task when such bits of news as came through were bad. He wrote letters by the hour, his steady hand racing over the paper with no sign of weariness. He wrote essays, interpreting his country; he printed and distributed them in quantity. He had countless visitors and through all his long days looked so confident that he began to get funds.

Wealthy Frenchmen called to offer money. Franklin wrote to the Secret Committee, "We are offered a loan of two million livres, without interest, to be repaid when the war ends." Beaumarchais, in London about his plays, collected money from friends of Franklin and other Whigs. With these funds, army surplus was purchased—uniforms, guns, and ammunition. But getting supplies to America was a major problem.

The long established three-way trade—England, West Indies, and the colonies—was changed now. American captains no longer sailed to English ports and paid heavy customs duties. They did business with merchants in Holland, or, when the English Channel was too dangerous, in Portugal, or Nantes, in France. Nantes was especially favored because it had long been a headquarters for the African slave trade; these ships carried guns because of pirates, and so there was an excuse for guns and ammunition in warehouses that might be visited by English captains. British spies were fooled for many months by this arrangement—planned by Franklin.

All this was complicated business. Most colonies had shipyards, but the nation had no navy—only hundreds of small ships busy in coastwise trade. Americans were eager to man these ships and face death or capture for their country and the chance of quick wealth in prize money. This trade centered in the free port of 'Statia in the West Indies, which was called, "General Washington's Arsenal."

"But we never keep our accounts balanced," Deane complained. "Here are three ships we've not heard from, though they've been gone months. Are they sunk—or captured?"

"We are not in a business where stock can be counted as a merchant counts goods on his shelves," Franklin reminded Deane. "Those ships we need, with indigo, rice, tobacco, or salt fish, may be at the bottom of the sea. Or captured by the British, or safely nearing a French port. Accounting must wait."

The whole year 1777 was difficult. Thomas Paine wrote a pamphlet, *The American Crisis,* and said, "These are the times that try men's souls." Without Washington at home and Franklin in Paris, the war might have failed. Yet lesser men tried to discredit these two patriots. Arthur Lee, torn by jealousy, tried his best to have Franklin dismissed; and a cabal against Washington nearly succeeded. Fortunately some men in high places and a majority of the people believed in them.

In Europe it became almost a fad to get to America and join the service. Men called at Passy begging for letters to Washington.

"We want to serve the cause of freedom," they said. Among these were Lafayette, Von Steuben, De Kalb, and other competent soldiers. How could Franklin be sure there was not, now and then, a dangerous spy? Franklin made no promises, wrote the vaguest of introductions, but managed to keep them all in good humor—some, he knew, would give priceless help to his country.

And America needed help. General Burgoyne was making a wedge between patriot forces in New York and New England. Howe was settled in Philadelphia. Fortunately, Franklin, in France, was having more success than his friends at home realized.

There was Captain Lambert Wickes, who sailed on the *Reprisal* from Nantes, captured five English ships, including a royal packet, and boldly sailed into the port at L'Orient, France, where he had no legal right to take English prizes. The ships were quickly sold, repainted, and set out. But before Wickes could get away, a cry was raised against him, and inspectors came. He pumped his hold half full of water and claimed the right of a distressed ship to stay and make repairs.

Captain Gustavus Conyngham, an Irishman, raided out of Dunkirk and insulted English shipping. France ignored these raids, proving that she was for the United States, not neutral, as she pretended.

These two men helped Franklin bring about the alliance with France. But he needed some dramatic good news from America to push the idea through.

Early in December, several patriots were with Franklin at Passy. Suddenly they heard the crunch of wheels on the gravel driveway. Deane rushed to the door as Jonathan Austin of Massachusetts climbed out of the carriage.

"Is Philadelphia really taken?" Franklin called to him.

"Yes, sir. Howe is comfortable for the winter," Austin said. Franklin turned back into the drawing room. For once his sparkle was gone. His clasped hands trembled.

"But wait, sir!" Austin ran up the steps. "I have other news. Burgoyne and his whole army were taken prisoners in October at Saratoga." The men fell upon him joyously, overwhelming him. Franklin went to his desk and picked up a pen. Friends of America must have this good news by the next post, because supplies from France had made the victory at Saratoga possible.

December, 1777, was a turning point in the affairs of the new nation. A messenger from Louis XVI came to Passy; the French government would make a secret treaty with the independent United States, provided the new nation would not return as colonies of England.

"It's a pity to have it a secret," Franklin said, "but once we get it signed, it may come to light sooner than the king expects."

Along with this good news, word came that cargoes of indigo, rice, and tobacco had arrived safely. The value was trifling compared with the huge debt to France. But the lift of spirits *some* payment made was enormous.

Franklin worked hours with Louis's representative, writing that treaty. It was not an easy document to arrange. Each nation must be pleased, and the translation must be accurate.

On February 6th the treaty was ready and the hour set for signing. For this occasion, Dr. Franklin wore the suit of brown Manchester velvet that he had worn for that painful trial before the Privy Council, in London. On that day he had been made to realize that England counted colonials as second-class citizens. He had been the target of shocking abuse and had heard the inspiring words—"A great republic." It is fitting, he thought, as he put the suit on, that I wear this when that republic, though struggling for life, signs a treaty with a first-class power —as an equal.

As he wrote his "B. Franklin" the thought came to him: this is the second important paper I am signing for my country. May all be well with it.

While others signed, his eyes took a final glance at the words of the treaty. Its tone was friendly, an agreement of alliance and trade; its thirty-one articles related to details of shipping and of how aid should be managed.

The king's determination for secrecy seemed to come from his fear that the congress might not sign, that England might still regain her colonies and leave France deserted. Dr. Franklin knew public announcement of that treaty would bring new life and hope to his country, so he did his best to persuade the king.

Then, quite suddenly, Louis agreed. A day in March was set and a reception arranged; the king would receive the American envoys and announce the treaty.

When Temple Franklin heard that news, he had a bit of business of his own. That done, he went to his grandfather.

"The wigmaker will call on you tomorrow, Grandfather."

"You know I will not wear a wig," Franklin retorted firmly.

"But for your country, Grandfather! Your friends all complain—you will not carry a hat. You will not wear a sword. At very least you can wear a wig."

"Why should I?" Franklin demanded.

"Because no man affronts a king by appearing in his own hair! Remember now, tomorrow at ten."

The wigmaker came. He measured; Dr. Franklin was meek and patient. On the morning of the great day, the wig was delivered.

"It is too small," Franklin complained, as it was put on his head.

"Impossible, sir!" The wigmaker was affronted. "My wigs are never too small. It is your head, sir; it is too large."

There was no time to argue. Franklin was dressed in new velvet, plain but handsome. Ruffles on his shirt were snowy white; silver shoe buckles sparkled—but that wig . . .

In the carriage, safely away from Temple, Dr. Franklin
jerked the uncomfortable thing off, tossed it onto the floor and
stamped on it, safely ruining its shape. Then he tidily smoothed
his gray hair—and appeared before the king, the most con-
spicuous man at the reception.

When they came away, the palace courtyard was packed with
people. As the Americans pushed their way over to the cabinet
house, the crowd shouted and applauded, showing vigorous
approval of news of the treaty.

This day's ceremonies, following the earlier secret signing,
marked a new feeling in France—as it would in the United
States when the treaty became known—a friendship between
nations, one the mighty France, under a king; one a small new
republic, but free. Many a Frenchman gave thought to that
contrast and watched more closely than before for news of the
United States of America.

The Treaty of Peace

 The alliance with France was celebrated in America, too. On the 6th of May, 1778, General Washington, the Marquis de Lafayette, and General Greene had the thrilling news read to their troops at Valley Forge. The cold winter was over; hope stirred that perhaps now the war, too, would soon end.

As for England, she could not believe that the United States would make an alliance with France. Was not England the mother country? During the following months several English envoys were sent to Paris, many chosen because of personal friendship for Dr. Franklin. These delegates offered everything once asked for—except independence, now held dearest of all.

After the alliance was completed, Franklin began trying to get American prisoners released. Because England did not recognize the United States as an independent nation, she did not consider captured Americans as prisoners of war. They were traitors to England and not worthy of humane treatment.

There has never been, nor ever will be, any such thing as a good war, or a bad peace.

Most of them were thrown into Old Mill prison near Plymouth or Forton near Portsmouth, England—cold, dismal buildings. A clergyman, Thomas Wren, who lived in Portsmouth, endeared himself to Americans by doing all he could for the men in Forton. He managed to get to them the eighteen pence, or sometimes a shilling, a week that Dr. Franklin gave or collected for them. Wren gave of his own small funds, too, and collected sums from Whigs in England. The prisoners' plight was still sad enough. At Old Mill matters were worse.

Not until well into the next year was Dr. Franklin able to set up a prisoner exchange. And even then there were never enough English prisoners for exchange.

A while after the alliance was signed, Silas Deane was recalled to report to congress, and John Adams was sent over in his place. Adams was loyal and intelligent, but set in his way; he did not try to adapt himself to the French. He was an important man in Massachusetts and in congress; he did not fancy taking the second place to Dr. Franklin that the French gave him.

"What the French see in Franklin, I cannot understand," Adams complained to his devoted wife, Abigail. "He dabbles in so many affairs, balancing all like a juggler with red balls."

"And the ladies he dines with are past enduring," Mrs. Adams added. "Not one would be invited to a party in Boston." A statement that likely was true. The Adamses never understood Franklin—nor his vast popularity.

Though Mrs. Adams did not see why women liked Dr. Franklin, Frenchmen did. He treated women as people. He listened to their ideas—in an age when women were not expected to have ideas. He was mannerly and gracious, and he always made his companion feel brilliant.

Among many, two French women were special friends; Madame Helvetius and Madame Brillon. Both were elderly women, well informed and good company. Franklin sometimes interrupted his endless writing of political letters to dash off a letter to one or the other. It was to Madame Brillon he wrote, on a very busy day, about a long ago incident of his boyhood:

"When I was a child of seven years old my Friends on a Holiday filled my little Pocket with Halfpence. I went directly to a Shop where they sold toys for Children and being charmed with the Sound of a Whistle that I met on the way in the hands of another boy I voluntarily offered and gave all my money for it. When I came home, whistling all over the house, much pleased with my Whistle but disturbing all the Family, my Brothers and Sisters and Cousins, understanding the bargain I had made, told me that I had given four times as much for it as it was worth, put me in mind of what good Things I might have bought with the rest of my Money and laught at me so much for my folly that I cry'd with Vexation and the deflation gave me more Chagrin than the Whistle gave me Pleasure.

"This however was afterwards of use to me, the impression continuing in my Mind, so that often when I was tempted to buy some unnecessary thing I told myself *Do not pay too much for the Whistle* and I saved myself much money."

He wrote on, telling his friend that he had met many people who gave too much for a whistle—a man who sacrificed friends and family joys for ambition; another who lost virtue for court favor; or comforts at home for saved gold; education and health for pleasure; goodness for passing satisfaction.

"These and others lacked my early disappointment by which I learned not to *pay too much for the Whistle.*"

Madame Brillon was delighted with her letter. She thought it exactly like Franklin—turning a humorous incident into a worthy moral. She begged him to print copies on his press so that she might give them to her friends.

Madame Brillon's enthusiasm, Franklin's amusement, and the copies did not please the Adamses. Perhaps this episode sent Adams hunting for the lease of the house at Passy. Monsieur de Chaumont owned the handsome house where Dr. Franklin, and now Mr. and Mrs. Adams, lived. Adams supposed that Dr. Franklin had leased the whole house, and he wanted Chaumont to move.

"But why?" Franklin asked, surprised. "It is his house."

"You have a lease," Adams said. "Why should he stay?"

"I have no lease," Franklin's eyes danced when he saw what Adams meant. "He's let me use his house."

"No lease!" Adams shouted.

"De Chaumont is my friend—and a friend of my country."

Adams tried to get a lease, but in vain. Monsieur de Chaumont and Franklin understood each other.

Adams complained to Arthur Lee. Their mutual dislike of Benjamin Franklin was a strong bond between them.

Life was painful and confusing for Arthur Lee and John Adams. Congress had sent them as envoys, as well as Dr. Franklin. Yet gentlemen from Paris, from Spain, from Holland, from England, always asked, "Is Dr. Franklin in? We wish to see him."

Usually Franklin was there—but likely as not in his tub. He suffered with gout and an occasional painful attack of bladder-stone. He got relief only by hot sitz baths. But sitting in a bath did not hamper Franklin.

"Who is it?" he would ask, when the doorbell jingled. If he knew the gentleman, he would say, "Show him right in."

"Of course there is a wooden cover fitted over most of the tub," Lee admitted to Adams. "But I fear it is more to hold the heat than for modesty—I really do." Life was not like this in Boston—nor even in Virginia.

The visitors never seemed to mind. They sat and talked —statesmen, or merchants, or shipbuilders. Dr. Franklin, ever a good listener, drew the towel around his shoulders; his hair dripped, and he smiled with relief from pain.

"It's abominable!" Mrs. Adams wrote home. "He should be recalled." But congress had no intention of recalling a man who was doing so well for his country. The bathtub was a long way off.

Then a little later, there was the matter of Temple Franklin —who begged congress to ask for his recall? Temple had finished his education and was acting as his grandfather's clerk when congress began asking questions.

"Is it right for an imprisoned Tory's son to be at the heart of American diplomacy in Paris?" The matter threatened to be serious—but Franklin refused to let it. Temple stayed.

To Franklin such matters were small things, hardly noticed. Congress wearied of the criticisms from Paris. They saw that three men should not have equal power and undefined duties. They appointed Benjamin Franklin Minister Plenipotentiary for the United States—putting him at the head of the group.

One of the reasons why Dr. Franklin was so busy was that he had the management of the fleet he was gathering—until he found John Paul Jones.

Captain Jones was Scottish, and he knew the coast of England and Scotland as he knew his father's garden. He was in France to get a commission. One day he chanced to be waiting at Passy for a clerk to bring papers on a French ship he had long been promised. He picked up a copy of *Poor Richard's Almanac* and thumbed its pages.

"If you would have your business done, go; if not, send," he read. At once he went to the palace; he got orders for his ship, which he named *Bon Homme Richard* in honor of the almanac that had inspired him to cut red tape and act.

In September of 1779, Jones, in the *Bon Homme Richard,* took the British *Serapis* in one of the most spectacular battles of the war. Dr. Franklin was happy about the victory, and thankful to have the English prisoners for exchange. The loyalty of those Americans in Old Mill and Forton had been well tested—the English had a standing offer of freedom to any man who would serve on a British ship. Ragged, cold, hungry as they were, those imprisoned Americans had a dream of freedom, matching the ideals of more famous patriots.

With Captain Jones's help in other captures, Dr. Franklin was able to free a good many.

The task of clearing and remanning prize ships taken also belonged to Dr. Franklin. Ship captains of many nations called at Passy begging for one of the few commissions congress had sent. Among these men was Irish Luke Ryan, captain of the *Black Princess* and a famous smuggler. The commission in his pocket, Ryan, aided by the *Black Princess* and *Fearnot,* sailed up into St. George's Channel to raid the shipping out of Liverpool.

In two seasons they took one hundred and fourteen prizes and many prisoners for exchange.

And so the years of 1779, 1780, passed, and 1781 was half gone. The United States was doing well on the sea and holding her own on land, but she had no decisive victory until late in that year, when France did her most spectacular service.

Lord Cornwallis was in the south, moving toward Williamsburg. Count de Rochambeau was with Washington in New York. Lafayette had skirmished with Cornwallis, when word came that Count de Grasse with the French fleet was in the West Indies. If he would come! If he would trap Cornwallis at Yorktown where reinforcements were expected . . .

Washington moved his forces from New York in record time. De Grasse gave up his plans in the West Indies, and at Washington's request spread his ships across the mouth of the wide York River. Lafayette, Rochambeau, and Washington moved together in such perfect timing that, on the 19th of October, 1781, Britain lost her entire army—seven thousand men— along with cannon, arms, and supplies.

No one knew better than General Washington the great debt his country owed to the French. He wrote to Count de Grasse:

"The surrender of York from which so much glory and advantage are derived to the Allies . . . belongs to your Excellency and has greatly exceeded our most sanguine anticipations."

Cornwallis's defeat shocked England.

"The war must end," men said. "It has been too long."

In France, in Paris, at Passy, there was rejoicing. Some were puzzled, too.

"How can so young a country be *free?*" they asked.

"Freedom! It would be good to be free of kings. We should go to America—soon." People called at Passy. More wrote to Dr. Franklin asking how to move to America. Finally, swamped by the requests, he wrote a pamphlet which Temple printed and mailed in reply to the letters.

As arrangements began for making the peace treaty, a new cabinet, more friendly to the United States, was formed in England. Congress sent John Jay to work with Franklin, Adams, and Henry Laurens, on the treaty committee.

Treaty making was tedious business. France thought England should give up Canada. England wanted Maine. And who was to get valuable fishing rights off Newfoundland? England insisted that colonial Tories should be paid for houses and businesses congress had taken—this was a bitter issue.

"No doubt England expects to pay the people of Falmouth, Boston, and other port towns, for damage done," Dr. Franklin remarked blandly—and the argument ended.

Then boundaries must be drawn in Florida, along the Mississippi, and between Canada and the United States. Franklin was the only one who noticed Isle Royale in Lake Superior. When he moved his pencil, giving it to the United States, no one objected. Perhaps only he knew that the island had copper that workers with electricity would need.

Preliminary agreements were signed November 30, 1782. Then work began on the formal treaty.

The long hours of conference tired Dr. Franklin. His mind
searched for diversion in the few free hours and found it in
the study of balloons. These lighter-than-air craft came into
vogue that year because one of the Montgolfier brothers sent up a
paper bag filled with smoke. Franklin followed the experiments
and wrote a report on them for the Royal Society.

"But what is the *use* of a balloon?" a friend, puzzled by
his interest, asked Dr. Franklin.

"What is the use of a newborn child?" Franklin retorted.

Another diversion was his study of simplified spelling. He
contrived a phonetic alphabet; he discarded many English spellings—for "gaol" he used "jail;" for "plough" he wrote "plow."
Later, these spellings became accepted in American usage.

Finally the treaty between the United States and England
was ready to sign on Wednesday, the 3rd of September, 1783.
For that ceremony Dr. Franklin again wore his suit of Manchester velvet. This was the third paper of state he had signed
for his country. Temple had the honor of sitting near, ready to
act as clerk if any last minute matter came up.

At the palace, the same day, Vergennes waited until a messenger brought word of the actual signing. Then France signed
her own treaty with England; and Spain and France signed
an "understanding."

His work done, Benjamin Franklin's thoughts turned homeward. But what about Temple? He was well trained for a
diplomatic post; the grandfather wrote requesting such a place
for the young man, now in his mid-twenties. He had served his

grandfather and his country faithfully—and without pay, though secretaries of other envoys had good salaries.

Months passed. No appointment came. Franklin's longing to see Sally grew, and his daughter wanted Benny at home. Passage was engaged, and plans made to leave.

During the interval after the signing, Franklin did some of his best writing. Among many essays were "The Savages in North America," "Higher Wages in Europe because of the American Revolution," "Luxury," and a new version of the pamphlet on "Moving to America."

To his father's surprise, William Franklin wrote from England, wanting to see Temple.

"Instead of answering, go over and see your father," Franklin suggested. "Better now than just as we leave."

"Perhaps he means to come here," Temple said, wondering.

Franklin did not suggest such a visit. Perhaps old hurts were too deep. So Temple went to England.

In 1785, Thomas Jefferson, the newly appointed minister, arrived in Paris, and Dr. Franklin was free to leave. Jefferson had his own high reputation in France because he had written the Declaration of Independence. But of all the Americans who had come to Paris during Benjamin Franklin's long stay, the Virginian had the highest appreciation of the older statesman. At a reception given for the two men someone rushed to greet Jefferson.

"So you have come to take Franklin's place," the man said.

"I come to succeed him," Jefferson answered gravely. "No one can take his place."

The Fourth Document

The decision to return to America was made; Mr. Jefferson was in Paris to take over duties—but departure was still delayed. Dr. Franklin's health grew worse, and he suffered terrible pain from bladder-stone. He could not possibly endure a coach ride to Le Havre. He could not even take the short drive to Versailles to bid the king and queen farewell.

Temple saved the day by an idea for comfortable transport.

"I have engaged a boat to take us by river to the port," he said. But as weeks passed and there was no rain, boat trips were cancelled. By midsummer, when Franklin was somewhat better and Temple had his mass of papers sorted and packed, not a boat was moving. But good word came from the palace.

The queen would like Dr. Franklin to use her own litter. "He can ride comfortably in it as it hangs between two mules." This thoughtful offer was accepted. The king sent a gracious letter and his portrait, surrounded by a double row of diamonds.

A wise man will desire no more
than what he may get justly, use
soberly, distribute cheerfully,
and leave contentedly.

So, on the 12th of July, 1785, Franklin and his two grandsons left Passy, the youths in a coach, Dr. Franklin in the litter. Monsieur de Chaumont and his two daughters, and other neighbors, went along and had supper at the first stopping place.

As the Franklins rode on, from village to village, their journey was a tour of triumph—scores, hundreds, came to pay honor to the doctor when he passed by.

At Le Havre they took a boat for Portsmouth, where they were surprised to see William. Many English friends, too, came down to see the party off.

The meeting with William had its pangs; he was bitterly against the United States. But they did some family business amiably. Benjamin signed over to William the debt England owed him from Braddock's day—perhaps William in England could collect something. William, in turn, assigned his New Jersey farm to Temple. And then the travelers boarded ship.

Once away, Dr. Franklin felt invigorated as he always did on the sea. His health improved. Friends had urged him to use this time to complete his autobiography, but his own story did not interest him. That work had been done for William, who was no longer interested in his father.

Instead, Franklin finished his studies of ocean currents, now illustrated with careful maps. He wrote an essay on ships and the wisdom of dividing off portions of the hull into watertight compartments. This idea came to him from the Chinese, but, as usual, his version was an improvement on the original thought. Then he made a study of the cause and cure of smoking chimneys; his essay had many new, useful suggestions.

On the 13th of September they sailed into Delaware Bay and sighted Philadelphia before evening. A fast rider had brought news of their ship; so Richard Bache came out to fetch them ashore. The wharves were packed with people who shouted greetings.

"They say my name!" Franklin exclaimed to Richard. "Is all this for *me?*" When Richard assured him, Franklin added, "I have few contemporaries to greet me. Do these others know how I have been criticized and derided?" He could hardly believe this ovation.

"Most Americans hold you in reverence for your service to our country," Richard replied. He was astonished, in turn, that his father-in-law would have doubted.

In his diary, Franklin wrote of his homecoming, ending with: "Found my family well. God be praised and thanked for all his mercies." A letter awaiting him from his beloved sister was a final joy in a happy day.

The next morning Franklin breakfasted with his grand-children—there were seven—and noted their good looks and bright ways.

"How fortunate that I came home!" he exclaimed. "I am done with politics, Sally. I shall stay right here and enjoy my family."

He had hardly said the words when a friend appeared with news.

"First thing this morning you were nominated as councilor representing Philadelphia for the state. We hope to elect you to head the commonwealth."

"But I am an old man!" Franklin protested. "I have just told Sally I'll have no more politics!"

"Forget your years, Ben. We need you. Our state is torn with strife between Conservatives and Republicans. Only a man with your gifts for reconciling opinions can save us."

Franklin could not refuse a duty, and with improved health, the service asked of him was possible. Election day was in October; friends urged him to serve his state. John Jay wrote that Franklin was the man to bring harmony. "If you accomplish this, much honor and many blessings will result."

Benjamin Franklin was a modest man. But he could not help feeling pleasure at this wide assurance of his countrymen's faith in him. The jealousies of the Lees and the Adamses, and his son's desertion, had shaken him more than he had realized.

He did not wish to intrude all this new business onto Sally's family, so he at once started building an addition to his own house. It was to be three stories; the first a large room for meetings or other gatherings, the second, a library and study, the third, his bedroom. In good autumn weather the work went fast.

Life quickly settled into a routine. Temple had gone to the New Jersey farm, now his own. He found he liked agriculture and stayed there. Benny went to New York to finish his education. And Dr. Franklin adjusted himself to a new secretary.

On election day "his Excellency Benjamin Franklin Esq. was duly elected President and the Honorable Charles Biddle, Esquire, Vice-President of the Supreme Executive Council of This Commonwealth." This office was the same as governor in some states.

By this time Dr. Franklin realized that life in his country had changed, and was still changing. The wilderness no longer hugged the town as it had when he first arrived more than sixty years earlier. Newcomers from Europe came almost daily and went on south or west. Travel became more usual, and mail went through quicker than ever before.

Shipping crowded old and new wharves. From the war's end, the pattern of American shipping changed. Captains no longer went only to the West Indies and Europe. Ships ranged the seven seas, taking American goods, returning with things Americans wanted. Franklin was happy to see that shipping he had fostered had grown; that larger, swifter ships were being built for longer, more daring voyages.

With all these changes on land and sea, patriots were finding that the rather loose Articles of Confederation of the 1770's were inadequate for a rapidly growing republic. The very prosperity of the nation brought new problems of government—the war debt, the relation of state to state, and of each to the central government. A firmer document was needed.

Back in war times, Alexander Hamilton, a young aide on General Washington's staff, had urged the making of a new and stronger constitution. Some approved, but many vigorously opposed his idea. Only after seven years of diligent work did Hamilton get action. A convention to make a constitution was set for May of 1787. Even then there was opposition. General Washington distrusted a stronger central government and had to be persuaded to be a delegate.

"We need you," friends told him. "And we need Dr. Franklin. The people trust you two; with your support we have a chance." So Washington accepted, and Dr. Franklin agreed to nominate him as president of the convention.

Delegates were slow in coming, so Dr. Franklin used the time to gather a few at his home for tea in the garden, or dinner. This way, he renewed old friendships and made new ones.

On the opening day, May 25th, such a terrible storm raged that Dr. Franklin was advised not to risk his health by coming to the State House. So Robert Morris was given the honor of nominating Washington. After that day, Franklin was in his place for five or more hours each day, during four months— always calm, always willing to listen.

Through the whole summer the delegates worked faithfully and in secret. James Madison had special knowledge of law and government; Hamilton, skill in administration. Almost every man played some active part. And through it all, Washington kept his temper and Franklin his smile.

Franklin favored one house in congress; he thought that a better balance between executive, judicial, and legislative could be had with one, not two, parts. His idea lost. The most vexing problem was the balance between large and small states. Virginia, Pennsylvania, and New York would not let Delaware and Rhode Island have power equal to their own. Franklin's suggestions of a senate with equal representation for each state and a house with representation according to population seemed the solution. Franklin had the idea that the president should serve without pay, but that was not approved.

Many excellent speeches were made. Franklin was not able

to stand long enough for speechmaking; he wrote his out, and his friend James Wilson read them. For this reason, all of his speeches were preserved in the record.

Afternoons Dr. Franklin invited guests to tea in his garden. Under a spreading mulberry tree, weary men could relax. Sally was a skilled hostess; the children were devoted to their grandpapa. Men found this a time when ideas mellowed.

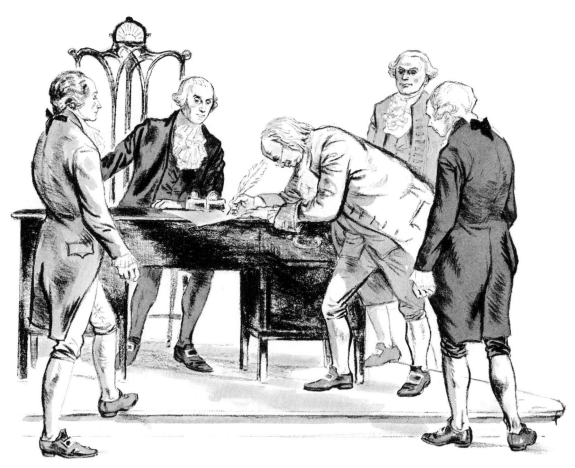

Finally, on September 17th, the constitution was ready for a vote. Dr. Franklin urged its acceptance.

"This document is not perfect," he said. "We may have to amend it as time passes. But we need a constitution. Let us accept it, and get on with our nation's business." It was accepted.

As men came to the table to sign, Washington leaned forward, and Franklin noticed the design of a sun, carved on the back of his chair.

"As we argued," he remarked to the man next to him, "I have wondered whether this design was of a rising or a setting sun. Now I have the happiness to know that it is rising." The accord of this final day did promise well for the country's future.

When his turn came, Franklin stepped forward and signed his name. This was the fourth great document connected with the beginnings of the nation, and Dr. Franklin was the only man who signed all four—the Declaration of Independence, the Alliance with France, the Treaty with England, and the Constitution of the United States of America.

For three annual terms Dr. Franklin accepted the office of president of Pennsylvania; then he retired to set his affairs in order and to enjoy his family. Not long afterward he had a bad fall in his garden and from then on, the bladder-stone gave him periods of terrible pain. In between, he had many joys with his family and with visits from friends. General Washington came to see him, and Mr. Jefferson visited him on a return from France.

The summer of 1789 he had an unexpected pleasure; Noah

Webster sent him a copy of his new book, *Dissertations on the English Language*—dedicated to Benjamin Franklin.

"Why does it have your name in the book, Grandpapa?" Sally's daughter asked. Franklin pointed to the dedication page.

"He says he liked my essay on spelling," Franklin paraphrased the formal wording. "Maybe you didn't know that I tried to help in your spelling lesson by making words spell as they sound?"

"Thank you for trying, Grandpapa," she said, and ran to play.

In the same year Franklin was well enough to write several excellent papers, one on the abolition of slavery and another on improving the condition of Free Blacks in Pennsylvania. And he made his will. His estate was something like $150,000—a considerable sum then; mostly in land or houses in Philadelphia and Boston. He also owned land in Ohio, Georgia, and Nova Scotia, and some bank stock—a wide range of interest for his time. He willed bequests to family and other relatives and considerable sums for education, a cause he had given generously to during his lifetime.

Amazingly, his good humor carried him through hours of misery, and he always had a smile or a joke for his grandchildren and their friends, who came and went in his room as though it were their own. Death came while he was sleeping, April 17, 1790.

Congress, which had not yet paid his salary and expenses for his service in France, declared thirty days' mourning and joined in the procession to his grave in the cemetery near Christ Church.

The newspapers reported it as the greatest procession ever seen in the city. Not long after, a bronze plate was put on the wall by his grave with the statement of his faith in immortality that Ben had written when he was twenty and so ill he thought he would die. It said:

The Body of
B. Franklin Printer
(Like the Cover of an old Book
Its Contents worn out
And stript of its Lettering and Gilding)
Lies here, Food for Worms.
But the Work shall not be lost,
For it will (as he believ'd) appear once more
In a new and more elegant Edition
Revised and corrected
by the Author.

The eighteenth century was a stirring time in history. New ideas abounded in the arts, in science and invention, in philosophy and government; great men of many nations led people's thinking into bold new channels. Among world leaders, Benjamin Franklin was the most versatile; he lived through most of this notable era, and he won acclaim on two continents.

A unique combination of talents lifted this unschooled son of a candlemaker to world fame: he had a lively curiosity combined with diligence and patience. Moreover, he had a passion for knowledge, a devotion to the service of his fellow men, a reverence for God.

Instead of using his abilities for his own gain, Franklin gave his inventions freely—his stove, lightning rod, insurance ideas; his writings, his skill as an advertiser, and countless other things which enrich our living to this day. He made his greatest gift when he turned aside from his loved work as a scientist to devote all his time and skill to the launching of a new nation, dedicated to the ideal of liberty and justice for all. To this struggling young nation he brought a sense of unity—a gift possible only from a man who knew every colony and who had long seen his country in perspective from across the sea.

After nearly two centuries, Benjamin Franklin continues to be loved and honored in his own country and in the world for his genius, his patriotism, and his warm humanity.

A List of Benjamin Franklin's Discoveries, Inventions, and Innovations

Aeronautics:
  Suggested aerial reconnaissance from balloons
  Proposed aerial bombardment from balloons

Agriculture:
  Advocated enclosing fields with hedges for wood conservation
  Introduced Scottish kale, Chinese rhubarb, Swiss barley, Newton pippin apples, yellow willow (for basket-making), Barbary barley, and turnips
  Promoted silkworm culture by sending silkworm eggs and mulberry cuttings from England.

Civic:
  Pioneered in street lighting, street cleaning, organized police, established fire company

Education:
  Organized the Junto, a club for promoting self-improvement
  Founded American Philosophical Society (for interchange of knowledge)
  Organized Pennsylvania Academy and College
  Organized The Library Company of Philadelphia (first subscription library)

Electricity:
  Developed single fluid theory, with positive and negative properties
  Electric ignition of gases
  Discovered electric repulsion
  Electric jack (motor)
  The lightning rod

Heat:
  Conductivity of heat by color
  Cooling by evaporation

Hygiene:
  Modern ventilation methods
  Theories on drafts

Inventions, Miscellaneous:

- Pennsylvania fireplace
- Stove
- Bifocal spectacles
- Remedies for smoking chimneys
- Depth of water in canal regulates speed of barges — drew up formulae for engineers
- Street lamp
- Washing mangle or wringing machine
- Copying machine
- Clock with three wheels

Medicine:

- Flexible catheter
- Co-founder of Pennsylvania Hospital
- Numerous articles with original contributions on lead-poisoning, common cold, etc.

Meteorology:

- Identified Aurora Borealis as electric phenomenon
- Cause of water spouts
- Movement of northeast storms

Military:

- Brought about establishment of militia

Music:

- Armonica (improved)

Navigation:

- Pouring oil on water to calm surface
- Charted Gulf Stream
- Watertight bulkheads for ships

Miscellaneous:

- Daylight saving
- Sundial with miniature gun firing at predetermined time